Don't Judge Me, I'm Only Human

Alecia Collins

Edited by Elijah Jean Editing.

Some names and identifying details have been changed to protect the privacy of individuals. I have tried to recreate events, locales and conversations from my memories of them. In order to maintain their anonymity in some instances I have changed the names of individuals and places, I may have changed some identifying characteristics and details such as physical properties, occupations and places of residence. Some names and identifying details have been changed and or omitted to protect the privacy of individuals.

DEDICATION

This book is dedicated to my dear mother Irma Joyce Collins and every young woman who's searching for acceptance.

Mother, I am so very proud to be your one and only daughter. You've shown me the true definition of what unconditional love means. A child of God you are and for that he has always covered your two children with his grace and mercy. Thank you for allowing me to make mistakes and to learn from them, without passing judgment. I will forever love you my Queen.

To my ladies, sisters, and friends, hold onto faith. Faith will pull you out and through some of the hardest times in your life. Always believe in yourself and never give up. Continue to love yourself for who you are. Last but not least, demand respect in every situation and show dignity.

PROLOGUE

To God be the glory. I am truly humbled and honored to have this opportunity to share my life experiences with my readers. About two years ago, as God began to work on me, my understanding was unclear as my life began to transition.

Throughout both my childhood and adult years, I've experienced shameful moments that did not make me proud. For many years, I carried hurt and pain which I kept covered with material items. Certain individuals were placed along my path to help me mature spiritually and professionally. Now, I have spiritually transitioned from what I once was to who I am today. I am a woman who holds her head high no matter what the situation may encounter. I am happy with what God has chosen for me and I plan on staying true to self and others.

INTRODUCTION

Families throughout the world experience harsh realities of life; many of which have a lasting impact within the family. These issues range from struggling with self-identity, mental health illness, to dealing with family in the prison system. In the black community, these are issues that we often encounter, yet seldom deal with.

For example, there are several households who deal with family members that suffer with mental illness; many of which who get thrown into society without the proper support. Those individuals lack the appropriate assessments and resources to deal with their disease, such as social service support agencies, medication, and psychiatric counseling, and therapy. This lack of resources coupled with government budget cuts makes it even more difficult for individuals who suffer with mental illness get the help they need. It's up to the family members to continue to fight for our love one's equal rights and stable wellbeing.

What many don't discuss is how these mental illnesses sometimes stem from life experiences such as struggling with self-identity. This is especially true for many women and young girls. Today, we as women have had our dignity to be stripped away from us. Sometimes we even go as far as selling our souls for material pleasures. It is this constant battle of discovering who we are. It is time for women of all walks of life to come together as *one* and assist with pulling one another up and encourage each other to do better as the women we are.

This also goes for our men. Society has painted this image of money and fame as the end all ,be all to be deemed successful. Unfortunately, the belief in this, is the reason many "minorities" are the *majority* who are sentenced to the prison systems. These men are sentenced to decades of years behind bars believing this dream—sadly, is went about the wrong way. Several of these individuals come from a poor upbringing and low income house hold. Because of this, they are desperate to make money, and the quicker the better. Because of these many end up in prison because of distribution of controlled substance. It is a cycle that our men know too well, and difficult to get out of; yet it doesn't end there. When they are released from prison and return to society they now carry the weight of being a convicted felon. This automatically decreases the opportunities for employment, financial stability and shelter. Because of this, stressors may arise which often affect their mental health.

The cycle has to end.

It is time for organizations and communities all over the world to connect with resourceful services to serve the community. It is time to end the stigma of mental illness, and end the cycle of recidivism. It is time to let our young girls and women know that they are born great. It is time to address these issues.

1
SUMMER OF 1990

I didn't think my life would be this way.

As a child, I always knew there was something different about me compared to other girls my age. Unlike them, I had to grow up fast. I didn't have the luxury of being a kid. At eight-years-old, I was an adult.

My name is Alecia Collins. I was born Aug 20th to Irma Collins and Jessie Hightower in Peoria, Illinois. I grew up in a single parent household with my older brother Steve. We have a four-year difference, but that hardly ever mattered—we stuck together like glue. Steve and I don't share the same father, something which was hard for people to believe because we favor each other. Steve's father was very much involved in his life; even though his father lived out of state it never interfered with them having a relationship. My dad on the other hand was always missing in action. When he would come around it wouldn't be for long, only to make promises that he wouldn't keep. As a child it bothered me, but as time went on I learned how to deal with it and not even care—so I thought.

Steve was the man of the house. He took care of mother and me. My mother was 'sick'. As kids, we were not aware that my mother suffered with mental illness; specifically, Schizophrenia. Unlike what we often saw in movies, my mother wasn't harmful to herself or others. She would just daydream and talk in circles. Unfortunately, her battle with mental illness inhibited her ability to keep a steady job, leaving Steve with the daunting task of caring for a family. He had to man up, so he did. It didn't make sense that my brother took on this fatherly role. I wanted us to play, Steve worried about what we would eat for dinner. I was too young to understand a lot of what was going on; yet, I had to learn fast. It seemed all our roles switched. Steve taught me how to wash dishes, fold clothes, clean. and cook. He was preparing me, so I wouldn't stumble along the way. What started as "fun lessons" became my daily way of living. Before I knew it, childhood escaped me. I was the woman of the house.

Our upbringing was different from other children we knew. We had no curfew, no chores, and no discipline whatsoever. Our mother gave us the freedom to do whatever we wanted. With no parenting, Steve and I governed ourselves. We were adults. Back then it all seemed normal; but as we became older we experienced how it changed our lives.

***

In the summer of 1990, mother packed us up and relocated the family to the north side of Peoria. That year I was going into the 2nd grade and Steve was entering the 6th grade. We had the entire summer to meet new friends and adjust to the neighborhood, but I knew it wouldn't take long to do so. Steve and I were both friendly; making friends would be a piece of cake for us. I grew up watching Steve connect with people from the neighborhood who would later become his buddies. His boldness was something I admired. Whenever he would come home I would ask "Do they have any sisters my age?" He would just laugh and I couldn't understand why because I was serious. Moving into this neighborhood, I knew that it would be no different.

Our new neighborhood—Madison Avenue—had many kids and was very diverse, the most diversity I was every accustomed to. Black, White, Hispanic, if you name it, most likely someone was from that culture. What made it even more unique was that everyone knew each other's families by names. There was no way you could get away with anything without your mom finding out about what you've been accused of. It felt like every mother on the block was your mom. There were a few live-in fathers in the neighborhood; most households were run by single mothers. Madison Avenue was a special street. It was filled with homes in all different shapes and sizes. Big and small colorful houses, some decorated with beautiful flowers and others with well-groomed lawns. The sound of barking dogs was indication that someone was home, or other should stay away. It seemed everyone had a pet. I fell in love with Madison Ave. it was a neighborhood with meaning and purpose. I knew it would be a memorable summer.

My second day in a new neighborhood already felt like home. I was ready to introduce myself to the neighborhood. Two houses down there was a kid who looked about my age. He had a bike that I will never forget. It was a red bike with chrome wheels and pegs. I walked pass his house and saw him outside popping wheelies on his shiny red bike.

Mesmerized by the chrome wheels, I don't notice that he was coming my way.

"Hey, my name is John. What's your name? He asked. He's wearing a white t-shirt, some shorts and some fresh Nike's. He must be the popular kid on the block, I thought.

"I'm Alecia," I responded in a low voice.

"Huh? I can't understand you," John replied.

"Alecia, Alecia Collins," I said in a louder tone. John smiled. Out of nervousness, I blushed. He looked over at his bike then turned back to me.

"Would you like to go bike riding?" he asked.

"Of course," I replied. Within minutes John got on his bike and I went to get mine. That conversation was the start to my first official friend on the block and boy was I excited.

For the next week John and I were best friends. Yet, that friendship ended as quickly as it started. For seven days straight, all we did was argue. We would pick fights about silly stuff such as who could run faster and who could kick the ball higher. This carried on for a full week until the seventh day. I quickly realized John was jealous of me. Although he was a boy, as a girl I had more freedom than him. I could ride my bike all day without checking in with my mom, he couldn't. In fact, John had a curfew. He had to be in the house before the street lights came on. I thought his mother was mean. It didn't make sense to me that John couldn't stay out to play with me. Even when I wanted to, most of the time, I was too terrified of her to knock on the door to ask for him. With all the freedom I had, John's lack of it became an easy target for teasing. I would tease him often. If it wasn't about his curfew it would be about other things. I would often refer to him as "Black Knight" because his skin complexion was charcoal black. I would playfully call him that but he hated it. On the 7th day of our friendship, he had enough. As soon as the words "Black Knight" left my lips, John smacked me across the face and ran me over with his bike. I couldn't believe he whacked me across the face. He must have lost his mind and I am sure he knew it. John crossed the line big time and he knew my brother wasn't having that.

"Steveeeeee!" I screamed to the top of my lungs. Steve was not only my brother, he was my bodyguard. John crossed the line and he knew Steve was not having it. Before I had time to explain what happened, Steve came running out the house. As soon as he saw me upset, he chased after John. Steve was a fast runner; however, John was on his bike. That day, even with his speed, he just couldn't catch John. Hearing our yells, my mother came outside to intervene. Her solution was simple, "Alecia, play with the girls." Just like that, my friendship with John was over.

I was, back to square A, 'searching for some girlfriends' as my mother would say. Later that day I decided to go bike riding through the neighborhood. As I rode pass a house on my block there was a young girl standing on the porch who looked about my age. Renee was her name. I invited her to go bike riding with me. She agreed but first she had to check with her granny to make sure it was okay.

Renee lived with her granny and the rest of her family. The first time I went over to her house I was at an awe. Her house was much different from what I was used to. As soon as you walked in you could tell her lifestyle was different. She had floor model TV's, VCR's, endless movie collection, and a stereo system that the whole neighborhood could probably hear. To top it off, her house was filled with food. Anything you could possibly want to eat, I'm sure she had it. Seeing all this, I knew Renee would become my new best friend. Her granny would always cook big meals. It was as if Thanksgiving was every day. As soon as you walked to her front door, the smell of fried chicken filled the air, so much so that you could taste the very spices that granny used. Granny's chicken was to die for and her home-made dressing was finger-licking good. Although Renee was my best friend, her Granny's food was more of the reason I wanted to play at her house rather than mine.

Unlike Renee, we rarely had big meals at home. When we did it would only be around the first of the month or when my mother had extra money. My mom couldn't work and was limited on funds so we had to make do with what we had. Although we did not have big home cooked meals as frequent as Renee, my mother would always say yes to anything my brother and I would ask for as long as she could afford it. She always provided for us.

My mother's heart was made of gold. She never saw any wrong in anyone. This was especially true when it came to our family. With such a big house, my mother allowed her niece and nephews to move in. Initially, it was a short-term arrangement. They would have a place to stay and help with bills, until they saved enough money to find their own place. Unfortunately, finding a place on their own never happened. Steve and I hated it. We pleaded with my mom to say no, and have them move out, yet our pleas did nothing. She would just smile and say "Not too long babies." 'Not too long' turned into weeks, and weeks turned into months. We knew they would take over and that's exactly what happened. What made it worse was their sticky fingers, they would steal and took the few electronics we owned. The once 'temporary' situation turned into a frustrating four years.

***

Weeks went by, and Steve and I began adjusting to the changes of our new home. I continued to hang out with Renee, but noticed that I no longer recognized Steve's friends. He had a whole new crew from the first group of guys he first started hanging out with. These guys weren't the familiar faces I was used to seeing Steve associate with. One day, he brought them into the house to introduce them to our mother while mom was pressing my hair out with the heating comb, getting me ready for Sunday school the next day. Steve's face lit up bright, as he introduced the guys one by one.

"Mom, these are a few guys who'll be attending school with me this school year, they don't live to far from our house." The boys waved and stepped up. "Kent, Greg, and Scott. Kent and Greg are first cousins," Steve said proudly introducing his new friends.

"Nice to meet you fellas," Mom replied. After the short introduction, Steve shifted his focus to me.

"Hey sis, come with me to Kent's house he has a sister about your age he wants to introduce you to."

"Mom, can I go?" I asked my mom, knowing she would say yes.

"Yeah, that's fine. But not until I finish combing this head of yours." I smiled in excitement being careful not to move too much, I didn't want to get burned by the pressing comb. I was finally going to make some new friends.

After about a half hour, Mom finally had my hair pressed out. With the summer heat, my thick hair would not stand a chance. Mom decided to slick it up into a sleek ponytail. It looked sharp. I threw on a change of clothes, and then headed out with Steve and his friends to Kent's house. Kent only lived about three blocks away from our house on a side street called Hayward Ave. When we arrived at the house, you could hear people from the inside of the house outside. Kent opened the door and we walked into a crowded room. There were so many girls my age and older sitting in the living room. It had to be over twenty people total in the house at one time.

"Hey Alecia, that's my sister over there getting her hair braided," said Kent. I looked over and waved. She was sitting on the floor as (who I assumed to be) her mother did her hair. She waved back and let me know her mom would almost be done her hair. A few moments later, her hair was completely braided and she walked over and introduced herself.

"Hi, my name is Alecia," I smiled and said.

"I'm Kissie," she replied. *Wow*, I thought to myself how cute of a name.

"Is that your real name?" I asked.

"No," she replied, "it's my nickname." We both laughed.

At eight years old, hearing someone my age with a nickname was new. My family always referred to me by my first name. This family was different from what I was used to. What fascinated me even more was the fact that so many family members were in the house, the majority being children. This seemed to be the place to be, and I made a point to always be there. I spent my entire summer at Kissie's and Renee's house. At Renee's I was guaranteed a hot meal and at Kissie's I was guaranteed some fun—that's where all the action was.

***

Before I knew it, summer was quickly coming to an end and we only had two weeks before class was back in session. Wanting to end our summer in style, my brother convinced my mother to host a house party. Over the summer, Steve became extremely popular so I knew this party would be a big deal. With his connections, this party meant that everyone from the north end of Peoria was invited. We knew once the invites were sent, getting people to come was easy.

After a week of planning, the day of the party finally came—August 8, 1990, a date I will never forget. The party started at 8pm. I was excited to attend but quickly became disappointed when my mom made me go to my room. She said I wasn't "old enough" to attend. It wasn't fair, but I didn't want to make matters worse so I went upstairs. I tried to lay down but the music was hard to ignore. I couldn't get sleep even if I wanted to. Using this to my advantage I went to my mom and complained. It didn't take much to convince her, with the blaring music, she had no choice but to let me hang out.

I watched from the top of our stairs as teenagers poured into our house in packs. Everyone, girls and boys, were dressed to impress. They were styling. Some of the girls wore their bright red lipstick along with their Salt & Pepper hoop-style earrings. The guys wore their Slick Rick rope chains around their necks and baggy clothes. It looked like a scene from the movie *House Party* starring Kid 'n Play. The DJ was spinning tracks and pumping up the crowd over the microphone; it was exciting to watch how he took control over the crowd with his imitation of the Sugar Hill Gang.

"I said a hip, hop, hippie to the hip, hip-hop, a you don't

stop rockin, Are ya'll ready?" the DJ said over the mic.

"YES," everyone screamed in unison.

"One, two, three," the record dropped, and at the first beat the room went wild. If you didn't know the song, it was best if you moved out the way. As if on cue, the crowd gathered and began to sing.

"JUMP, JUMP! Kris Kross will make you, JUMP, JUMP!"

Everyone bounce up and down, waving their hands and shaking their hands. Even the girls that seemed 'too cute' couldn't help to participate in the frenzy. My face lit up from the excitement that was happening. The music had everyone's adrenaline racing. Sweat dripped from foreheads and the vibrations of everyone jumping pulsated through the floor, I could even feel it upstairs. I knew then, that this party was going to be one for the books.

It was official. My big brother was the talk of the North-end of Peoria. After the party, everyone knew Steve, which also meant that everyone now knew me. Wherever I went, someone recognized me, even if I had no idea who they were. In their eyes that didn't matter. All that mattered was that I was Steve's little sister.

***

School officially resumed. Unlike other students, I didn't get new clothes for the school year. This didn't bother me too much because I was used to it. Mom didn't have money so I just always made sure my clothes were clean and ironed. Those lessons Steve gave started to pay off. Despite not having new clothes, I was optimistic about the new school year. Second grade would be a piece of cake because I knew everyone in my class. They were all kids that I met from the summer. If I didn't know them all, they knew who I was. School days seemed long, but I made sure I went every day to enjoy breakfast and lunch. I didn't spend as much time as Renee's grandma house so I always made sure to eat at school.

Steve got out of school earlier than me. Because of this, everyday our mother would send him to meet me at the bus stop. At first he was always on time, however as time went by he would get later or not come at all. One day, I waited for a few minutes but he never showed up. So I proceeded to walk home. Our house was only a block away from the bus stop so I didn't think it was any biggie for me to be alone. When I arrived home my mother looked furious as soon she realized Steve wasn't with me.

"Where's Steven, Alecia?" She firmly asked. My mouth felt glued shut. Steve and me never snitched on each other and I wasn't going to start then. Instead of telling her the truth I simply and instantly replied, "Outside Mom".

Steve was hanging out with Kent and the guys. He began hanging out with them more than usual. One day over at Kent's house, I witnessed all the excitement and commotion they had going on. Although Kissie's house tends to have heavy foot traffic, something seemed different—especially with Steve. He looked like he was up to something unusual. There were rumors Steve would hang around Morton Square Park. I never believed it because that area was known for drug activity. My brother couldn't possibly be involved in that, *could he?*

That evening, my cousin Frank barged through the house screaming and yelling to my mother. I was sitting on the couch eating dinner and doing homework.

"You better get a hold of that son of yours before he goes to jail," cousin Frank yelled. "He's selling drugs."

Drugs? what does that mean? I thought to myself. My mother must have been thinking the same because she remained nonchalant, and ignored cousin Frank's discovery. She never brought it up again.

Months went by, and the holidays quickly approached. Christmas was always exciting even though we never got much. Thank God for my Aunt Wanda. We were her favorite niece and nephew so every year she made sure to load us up with gifts.

"Ho, Ho, Ho," my brother shouted as he came in the house. His hands were filled with bags of shoes, clothes, food, and candy. I was in awe. *Where in the world did he get the money to buy all of this?* Even at eight years old, I knew something didn't add up. However in that moment, it didn't matter where Steve got it from or how. All I knew was we were balling and I would finally get the chance to go to school with new shoes and clothes. Boy was I happy! Our mother felt otherwise.

"Steve, where did you get this stuff from?" Mom asked sifting through the bags.

"From Granddad," he answered looking my way. The look in his eye let me know he was lying. "I got in contact with my dad, and he wanted me to stop by to pick up my Christmas package."

It sounded believable. Steve's dad and grandfather always made sure Steve had a great Christmas and birthday, so something like this wouldn't be out of character. However, I couldn't help to recall what cousin Frank yelled months ago, 'Steve is selling drugs.' With that in my mind, this story that Steve told our mother was hard to believe. It was then I knew what my cousin Frank had said, may had been true.

Steve was hanging out at Kent's more often than usual. To make suspicions worse, Kent's family were well known drug dealers, which meant Kent was part of the 'family business.' Steve became more and more suspicious. Only in second grade, there was so much that I didn't quite understand, but the proof was there. Once I saw that bag full of gifts I knew what cousin Frank said was true. Steve was a drug dealer. From that day forward, my life completely changed.

2

THE ONE FOR ME

Ten years later, I was now in my junior year of high school with only one year left before I graduated. I couldn't wait.

I had it all, job, money, a car and the perfect boyfriend who had tons of cash. His name was Terrance and he was from Chicago. He was nine years older than me and called me his 'queen'. He was one of those 'boss type brothers' who kept me laced with the hottest clothing and jewelry. Terrance was a street dealer. Truth be told, that's what attracted me to him. By this time my brother was a heavy street dealer so I knew how much money was involved in the game. Being a drug dealer didn't faze me, it made me want Terrance more. To add to the attraction was his overwhelming good looks. He was a head turner. He stood at about six feet tall, and had a light chestnut complexion. He always smelled good and looked sharp. Although he was a street dude, Terrance was a gentleman. He was thoughtful and attentive which attracted me even more. Terrance and I met at work, at Apac Telemarketing Services. We often spoke and found out we had many similarities. Both our families were from Chicago and we both grew up in low income. He knew about the struggle as did I. The more we talked the stronger the connection felt. We were on the same page. He had the same drive as me. He wanted more out of life and would do whatever it took and by any means necessary to get what he wanted. We were a perfect match. With Terrance by my side, it seemed everything was falling into place.

Steve and Terrance never cared for each other; my brother always had a problem with Terrance age. We often argued about it. Steve didn't trust Terrance or his intentions. I was in love and I refused to let Steve get in the way. After about a year and half, I decided to move out. Steve was furious; however, I could no longer deal with his bickering. I was an adult and he was not going to stop me. Terrance and I got our own apartment in Peoria. Moving in together seemed to be the best thing that ever happened to me. We was in love and I was in paradise.

Things were going great. Six months into the time we moved in together, I decided to leave sales an pursue another career. After long days of studying I earned my certification in Pharmacy Tech and accepted a position at CVS pharmacy. I was so excited and knew this was a great opportunity. As time went on, the demands of work increased. My days were long and tiring. I worked almost six days a week from 11am to 7pm. My schedule took a lot of time away from our relationship. We barely spent time with each other, but Terrance understood my passion for my new position. When I arrived home he would always make sure to be waiting on me with something good to eat. I always looked forward to it, and knew even after a long day at work I would be with my man. However, one day that all changed.

I arrived home from work looking forward to a good meal. Terrance usually prepared a delicious dinner to eat by the time I came home. However, this night was different. There was no warm meal waiting and there was no sight of Terrance. The house was quiet.

Ring Ring, my house phone rang.

"Hello," I answered.

"This is an anonymous tip. Your so called boyfriend is at 2315 Wallace St," the person on the other end of the line responded.

What the hell, I thought. I instantly hung up the phone and a rush of anger consumed me. Questions raced through my mind as I tried to understand what just happened. Who the hell was this woman? How in the world did she get my phone number? And where the *fuck* was Terrance ass at?

Immediately, I called Terrance's phone. There was no answer. Panicking, I searched frantically for my car keys. When I couldn't find them I realized that Terrence had it. I was going crazy so I called Kissie to give me a ride. Within a couple minutes Kissie was outside.

"What in the hell is going on, Alecia?" Kissie asked, as I got into her car.

"This motherfucker, Terrance, has the audacity to be at another woman's house in my car! He be swearing to me he 'only loves me', and saying 'we going to get married soon'. He's making me look like a fool in these streets. I swear I'm going to kill this nigga," I said. Kissie didn't ask any more questions. She knew I was angry. After a couple minutes we pulled up to the broad's house. The first thing I noticed was *my* car parked outside her house. I couldn't believe Terrence. The sight of my car infuriated. Without thinking I jumped out of Kissie's car.

"Kissie, pop your fucking trunk." Her trunk popped open and I reached in to grab her crow bar. I walked up to the car in the driveway and lunged the crow bar over my head. The sound of glass shattering ignited the flame in me even more. With every swing of the crowbar, glass glazed the driveway ground. I hopped onto the hood of the car and swung with all my might. This bitch was going to suffer. Kissie pleaded for me to stop. Knowing that Terrance was inside that woman's home angered and hurt me bringing me into a rage that could not be controlled. I couldn't just stop.

"TERRANCE! BRING YOUR FUCKING ASS OUTSIDE. HOW DARE YOU. I'M GOING TO FUCK YOU UP AND THAT SLIMY BITCH!" I screamed. Swings happened between screams, and when I realized he wasn't coming out my swings became stronger. Police sirens started in the distance and I could hear them get closer.

"Alecia, we have to go, NOW" Kissie said while forcing me back into the car to leave.

***

When we arrived back at my house, emotions took over and waterfalls drenched my face. *How could he do this?* I thought. This was the beginning of a nightmare for me. The man who I loved more than anything was cheating and I caught him in action. As I sat patiently waiting for Terrance to come home, angry thoughts bombarded me. Hurt transformed to rage and more than anything I wanted to damage him like he hurt me. Sitting on the couch, I suddenly got up and Kissie followed suit. I went into the bedroom and ripped his clothes out of the closet.

"Kissie, go grab the bleach."

Without hesitation, Kissie, went into the kitchen and brought back the Clorox bottle. A smile spread across her face as she handed me the bleach. She was just as upset as I was and wanted revenge. I assembled the clothes in the middle of the bedroom and emptied out the bottle of bleach completely over it. I watched as his jeans began to fade as color stripped away from his tops. We laughed and gave each other high fives. *Fuck him*, I thought. Kissie, let me know she couldn't stay so I walked her back to her car. When I walked back in the smell of bleach took over. I went to our bedroom still furious when I heard the door shut loud. His footsteps approached the bedroom and when he saw his damaged clothes his mood swiftly changed.

"What in the hell, Alecia? Why would you do this shit?" he asked. The expression on his faced looked demonic but I didn't care. I wanted him to feel my pain.

"Yea, nigga what the fuck you going to do? " My boldness pushed him over the edge. He charged at me and in one swift move, he grabbed me by my neck and threw me onto the floor. I tried fighting him off but he held me down until I could no longer move. I laid on the floor and looked up at the ceiling, unable to fight back. I felt dizzy and heartbroken. I looked him in his eye and didn't recognize the man that stared back at me. I thought to myself "Could *this* be called love?"

The next day he flooded me with gifts and flowers and apologies upon apologies.

Yes. Yes, this was love.

***

A year went pass and things with Terrance spiraled downhill. Terrance gave me everything and more so I tried to keep the tension down. I began to allow certain things to go unnoticed to avoid conflict. Yet, the more I turned a blind eye, the worse he became. Terrance's infidelity was at an all-time high. Our regular trips to Chicago became lonely. During most of our visit Terrance would be gone and leave me in the house with his sister. The other half I would be sleeping. There was nothing I could do to get his attention anymore. The only attention I seemed to get was when he was under the influence, and that attention was not what I wanted—he would grope me in ways that made me uncomfortable. What once used to be a sweet, attentive man was now a man I no longer knew.

One day after returning home from a weekend in Chicago, I felt sick to my stomach . I was feeling dehydrated and Terrance told me I looked fatigued. He took me to the E.R. to get checked. What I discovered was a shock to us both. I was sixteen weeks pregnant. News of the pregnancy had me elated. This was the answer to our issues—a baby. Maybe this would possibly change the way our relationship had been going. For the first time in a long time we were both overcome with joy. After our doctors visit, we shared the news with our friends and family. We were going to be parents. I was going to be a mom.

***

My first check-up was scheduled shortly after the pregnancy test. With this being my first pregnancy, Terrance and I were extremely happy. We both hoped for a girl since Terrance already had two boys. When we arrived at the Doctor's office, the receptionist checked us in as we waited patiently. I felt nervous and doubtful. Now I know some may say this should have been one of the happiest days of my life, but it wasn't. So many thoughts and unanswered questions were running through my head. This man had cheated on me with multiple women in my house and car. *Will a baby actually make him change?*

"Alecia Collins." The receptionist called my name snapping me out of thoughts. I went into the check-in window and provided her with my insurance info. As she continued to check me in, I went back to sit back down. As I glanced over at Terrance from the corner of my eye, I could see him texting non-stop on his phone. I didn't want to start fussing at him since we were about to hear the good news about our new edition to the family, so instead I sat patiently waiting for my name to be called. Moments later a nurse came out and called me into one of the exam rooms. Terrance and I proceeded to head down the hall following the nurse towards the exam rooms. Going down the corridor, the walls were decorated with portraits of newborn babies with both their mother and father. The families in the picture looked so happy and in love. I couldn't help but to envy them. As I past each photo, doubts about my own relationship began to take over. *Would I experience a loving family like these photos portrayed* .I didn't want to be a statistic raising a child on my own. I experience that life—my mother raised me and my brother on her own. I didn't want that for my child.

"Okay, Alecia, here's your exam room. Please get undressed from the waist down. You may leave only your socks on. The doctor will be in shortly," the nurse instructed. She then left out the room and left me and Terrance alone.

I turned my back to Terrance and started to undress. When I turned around to face him he blurted out "I love you, Alecia."

My face glowed. I felt the sincerity in his voice and in that moment it was what I needed to hear.

" Terrance I love you," I responded.

Knock, knock.

"Come in," I replied. The door opened and in walked the doctor and another nurse.

"Hi, I'm Dr. Boyd and this is Nurse Yang who is here today to assist with your exam." I waved at Nurse Yang and she waved over at Terrance but he didn't notice because he was on his phone.

Dr. Boyd proceeded to prepare me for my ultrasound.

"So, what are you two hoping to have, a girl or boy?" Dr. Boyd asked.

Before I could respond, Terrance quickly popped his head up and yelled "A girl Doc, I already have two boys."

"Me too, Sir. Me too," Dr.Boyd said as he laughed amused by Terrance's enthusiasm.

As I laid on the exam table, Dr. Boyd moved the monitor around my stomach to check for our baby's heartbeat. I anxiously waited to hear it myself yet no sound came from the monitor. The jovial smile that was on Dr. Boyd's face began to fade. He looked at Nurse Yang and I felt the room close in.

Something was wrong.

"Nurse Yang, draw two tubes of blood from Alecia, now please," Dr. Boyd instructed. He took of his gloves and said he would be right back and stepped out. A heavy weight burdened heart.

"Is something wrong with my baby?" I asked as my voice choked. I looked at Nurse Yang frantically searching her face for answers. "What's wrong?" I repeated. Tears poured out my eyes and I felt my heart pounding vigorously.

"Alecia, please relax so I can finish drawing the blood that Dr. Boyd needs," she said attempting to calm my nerves.

Terrance stood up and came next to me, taking my hands in his. Nothing was making sense.

"What is going on with my baby?" I asked again.

"Take a deep breath, Alecia. Take a deep breath and relax," Terrance said in his attempt to console me. He repeated this continuously while Nurse Yang finished drawing my blood. After what seemed like hours, Dr. Boyd walked back into the room and took a seat next to me.

"Alecia, have you noticed any bleeding in the past few days or felt nauseous?" He asked.

"No, Doctor," I replied while I wiped the tears rolling down face.

"Why are you asking that, Doc?" Terrance asked.

"I do apologize to you both but from the results of your ultrasound you have miscarried. I'll leave you two sometime to cope with this," Dr. Boyd said. He offered his condolences and stepped out of the room. What were streams of tears turned into an outburst of cries. Terrance pulled me up and held me tight.

"Its's okay. It's going to be okay," he said. I didn't believe him. How could this turn out ok. The sight of the doctor's office sickened me. I was ready to go home. I lost my baby.

***

About six months passed since the miscarriage of our baby. The lost weighed me down and took a toll on my mental health. I took some time off work to regroup and make myself a priority. Terrance still went to Chicago every other weekend to handle business as usual while I stayed back to care for me. It was the summer and his old neighborhood had parties going on almost every weekend that he could not seem to miss. One day he returned home with exciting news. The upcoming weekend was going to be special because he planned a weekend of festivities for us at Navy Pier. It was June 7th, a day I would never forget. That day the sun was shining brighter than it ever was. The rays beamed off our skin highlighting our golden brown skin and the twinkle in our eyes. That day, the love between us glowed; it was at an all-time high—yet, for some reason it felt strange.

We headed downtown to start our day. Terrance stopped over his brother's house, who insisted us to try out the motorcycle and enjoy the day's cool breeze. We agreed and let him know that we would be back in a couple hours. Hopping on the motorcycle we went on our way. It was perfect. Riding on the Dan Ryan Highway, my hair was blowing in the wind, and my diamonds were shining on my neck and wrist, which were wrapped tight around Terrence. I was finally spending some quality time with my sweet heart in the beautiful downtown Chicago—what more could a girl ask for? It was a perfect day. When our date ended, we headed back to Terrance sister's house, where we would usually stay when we came into town, to freshen up for the evening. We veered up the highway on a romantic high not knowing that darkness was upon us both.

***

What is going on? I thought as I struggled to open my eyes. Overly drugged up, loss of sight, the pain was unbearable. It seemed I had entered a new body. *Where was I?* There were no familiar faces around, just white clouds. I was lost and

31

without answers. I started drifting and felt a transition from my living body to my spiritual body. I was only eighteen years old, I wasn't ready to die. "My life isn't complete yet," I said. Tears rushed out and I laid there and cried. "Why me?" I asked. What about my family and friends? They will miss me dearly. What about Terrance? Questions poured out but there were still no answers. My understanding was unclear as I began to weep and then a voice said unto me "You no longer have to cry."

A deep breath came from under me as I opened my eyes to see my family hovering over me in tears.

"Nurse, Nurse," my mother yelled.

"What happened to me?" I screamed. "What happened to my hand?"

I had nearly lost my mind looking down at my hand. "My thumb, my thumb! What is wrong with my hand?" My thumb was nearly detached from my hand and two of fingers had two deep lacerations. " Oh dear Lord, help me," I cried. The pain was unbearable and my screams became louder with the more blood I saw covering me. Everyone tried to calm me down but with no success. My screams only got louder and more erratic. I was living in a nightmare. A sharp pinch took me by surprise and before I knew it the weight of my eyelids became too much to keep open.

I awoke to the sound of Steve's voice. As my eyes slowly opened, things were still unclear. *Why was I in the hospital?*

"Alecia, you were in a motorcycle accident. You and Terrance were hit by a truck on the highway," my brother informed me.

"Where is Terrance?" I nervously asked. "Terrance, Terrance," I repeated longing to hear back his response. I was in so much pain yet all I wanted was Terrance.

"Alecia, relax. He's ok. Terrance is in the Intensive Care Unit. He broke his collar bone and damaged his rib cage, but he's okay Alecia. He had to have a several number of surgery procedures. We're just glad you are alive. You were in a coma for five days," Steve explained.

Five Days? I thought. I was in a comma for five days, my fingers were chewed up and Terrance had surgery. An accident? How did this all happen? Our day was going perfect just moments ago, yet Steve just said it was five days ago. It was too much to deal with. Only thing I could do was thank God for sparing us both from the horrific accident we encountered.

"Alecia," my brother said pulling me back to reality. "I'm going to head down to the cafeteria to get something to eat would you like a sandwich?" he asked. I could see in Steve's eyes how upset and sad he was. His face was red with worry; yet, he was there to make sure I had everything I needed. I don't know what I could do without him.

"No Steve, I'm fine," I responded. Steve walked out and a Doctor walked in. He reintroduced himself and let me know his name was Dr. McNabb, the skin graphing specialist.

"Hi Alecia, I am glad to see you are awake. How are you feeling today?" He asked.

"I don't know Doc, this has been so much. I don't even know where to begin," I said.

" I can understand this is a lot. I have some news for you. I have been examining and studying your arm case for the past three days, and have finally come to a decision on a treatment option," he said. The feeling was unbearable and the room was silent. "The good news is we do not have to amputate." Tears of joy poured out my eyes. *Thank you Jesus,* was all I could think. However, by the look of his face he wasn't finished.

"Unfortunately, you have lost an extensive amount of skin from your hand and arm. Because of this we must prepare for a skin graphing," Dr. McNabb said. I wasn't sure what he meant by "skin graphing" but I was happy I wouldn't have my fingers removed. Dr. McNabb went on about the graphing and what options I had. He explained that skin graphing was basically removing skin from one part of my body, and transplanting it to another part, in this case my wounded hand. When I heard this, I closed my eyes. *Transplanted skin?* I thought. My mind rushed with thoughts of how horrible this was but then I realized I would get to keep my hand. My eyes reopened with assurance that Dr. McNabb just saved my hand and my insecurities.

"So, when will this procedure take place Dr. McNabb?" I asked.

"In two weeks. Until then, we need to keep your thumb clean 24 hours a day which means three dressing changes daily as well as a daily antibiotic. This will help to fight against infection," he said. He gave me some more details for the procedure and left the room.

This was a lot to process but I was thankful. Transplanted skin is better than amputation

***

Terrance was released two weeks after the accident and spent most of his day in the hospital visiting me. We would spend the day rubbing cocoa butter and triple antibiotic on one another's scars and wounds. I often laughed to myself as the scent of those ointments spread profusely throughout the room.

Finally, the day for my surgery was here and Terrance was there to support me. I was so happy to have him with me while I went through surgery. There is no way I could have done this alone. I heard a knock on the door and knew it was time.

"Come in," I answered. The door knob twisted open and in came the surgery team.

"Alecia Collins, are you ready?" one of the doctors asked.

"Yes," I responded. My body had the jitters. I was nervous and hungry. The night before I couldn't eat or drink anything after 8pm so my stomach was empty. No fuel to keep me going just anxiety. Thankfully Terrance was by my side assuring me everything was going to be okay. He gave me a kiss on my forehead and I smiled as the surgery team wheeled me out the room.

"All right then, we are ready for action," Dr. McNabb said. I prayed to myself for all to go well as I was wheeled into the surgery room—alone.

My life felt only borrowed. The questions continued and my mind kept racing. Why I lord, why give me another chance? The lights in the operating room were bright. With my eyes, I traced the IV line which was running into my arm. I watched as the fluid dripped into the bag and into my veins. There was a lot of movement around me but all I could hear was "drip, drip, drip". As the IV distracted me, I was stuck with a needle in my back by the anesthesiologist. With no warning, I knew time was all I had on my side; and eventually the clock stopped ticking.

Hours later I woke up from the superficial surgery procedure that left the left side of my waist looking deformed due to the skin removal for my arm and hand. Terrance was the first person I saw in the recovery room. It felt so good to know he was there with me; especially after all we had gone through with the accident. I was taken back to my room where my family and friends were waiting. The love was so thick in the air you would have thought I just won the lottery. Everyone was so happy to see me. Eventually the day became short and everyone headed out one by one. At the end, my love Terrance was the last one standing behind.

***

With only a week left before I was discharged, Terrance needed to make a drop back in Peoria. This bothered me. I may have been trippin', but I wanted Terrance with me all day, every day. Of course, we all need air but I felt he was responsible for putting me that position.

"Alecia," Terrance said, "I need to get back to Peoria and check on my money. I'll be back in the morning." As he walked out the room, feelings of frustration stirred up.

"Don't fuck up!" I yelled behind him. He stopped, turned around and looked at me puzzled. He must've understood what I meant because in a low voice he responded, "I won't."

The next morning came and as usual the nurse came into my room to change my hand and arm bandage dressings. To wake up every day knowing your dressings had to be changed was torture. Every day I had to go through having my arm cleaned and checked for infections. Mentally, I was never prepared, especially seeing how deformed my hand looked. Only faith was able to help me through those moments to endure and overcome my anxiety.

The day had gone on and still no Terrance. I called his

phone over twenty times and each time there was no answer. The next morning Terrance walked into the room. I could see all over his face that he was fixing to lie and give me an excuse as to why he did not answer his phone. For about thirty seconds the room was quiet, but I couldn't hold it in any longer.

"Where in the hell have you been?" I yelled.

Silence.

"I know you hear me talking to you Terrance. What the hell? I'm laid up in this hospital bed 200 miles away from my family and this is how you treat me," I yelled.

Still no response from Terrance.

Just like that, the pain he had put me through for the past two years resurfaced. I always believed he would change. When the motorcycle accident occurred, I believed his love for me would mean more. Silly me, I was wrong once again.

The day came to check out of the hospital and I was excited. After spending two long months in a place with complete strangers, I was ready to go home. I got dressed and Terrance collected my things. As we were leaving the hospital Terrance told me he had a surprise waiting for me. Still upset from the night before, I gave him a blank expression. This didn't faze him as he always knew how to put a smile on my face, so I wouldn't be upset with him for long. We pulled up to a shopping plaza where we usually shop which had all my favorite stores. Before I could get out the car he reached over and grabbed my hand while holding a black box with a red ribbon in the other. "Open it," he said, smiling. I rolled my eyes and reach for the box. When I opened it, I couldn't hide my approval. It was a new diamond Movado watch. It was two toned with silver and gold and had diamonds encrusted into the bezel with the signature Movado dot. It was gorgeous. No matter how upset I was moments earlier, I couldn't deny its beauty. A grin spread across my face, but my heart was still broken.

This man knew all the moves to pull out his back pocket; although I was young, I was not foolish. The feeling of dragging my frustration on would only be depressing and with all I had going on from the accident, there was no room for it. I decided to give Terrance a pass and swept it under the rug.

***

Two full weeks passed since I returned home and per my physical therapist my arm was progressing quicker than normal. Since I lost all movement in my hand, I was to attend therapy twice a week. At 18-years-old I felt like a baby learning my motor skills all over again. It was one of the biggest challenges I ever faced, however my spiritual relationship helped made a difference. I would pray two to three times a day thanking God and expressing how grateful I was of Him for sparing my life and instilling strength in me. As small kids, my brother and I grew up in the church home. I always had that spiritual connection and even though I wasn't regularly attending services the spirit always formed through me.

As I sat on the couch going through some mail and dusting around the house, I was interrupted with a phone call.

"Hello," I answered.

"Yea, is this Alecia?" the other voice said.

"Yes, who is this?" I asked as I felt my anger developing.

" Yea, Terrance had me in your house when you were in the hospital."

Click.

I stood there speechless and felt my body become numb. *In my house?* I thought to myself. "Aww HELL NAW! In MY HOUSE while I was laid up in the hospital fighting for my life," I heard myself yell out loud.

My adrenaline was rushing. There was nothing this man could say or do to calm me down from this bull crap. Pacing back and forth I waited for him to walk through the door. This was the last straw. I knew it was time for me to put him out my house.

When he came home, I completely lost it.

"GET OUT. GET OUT OF MY HOUSE" I screamed. With no response Terrance immediately grabbed me in an attempt to calm me down.

"It's not true, it's not true," he pleaded.

In between his pleas, his lips found mine, and his kisses quieted me. He embraced my body relieving the very pain he caused. In moments the conversation went from "get out" to romance.

Terrance had no clue what I was accusing him of but he knew how to shut me up. His lies and abuse were covered with gifts and sex. Nothing could make me see differently, I was blinded from the truth.

3

A NEW ATTITUDE

A new year was approaching and I would soon be nineteen years old. Terrance and I just bought a new car, we had plenty of money, and I even had met a few new girlfriends. Life was amazing. I began to club every weekend at *Club E*. Although I wasn't twenty-one, I carried myself like a lady at all times which always made me seem of age. The more I showed my face the more I began to get noticed by a different crowd of men. My friend Ria knew everyone—all the ballers, the broke ones, and who to stay the hell away from. The idea to cheat on Terrance never crossed my mind but I knew if I did, it had to be with a brother who kept plenty cash. There was no such thing of 'stepping down' to a low budget guy; especially, when you are used to an upbringing with a brother and a man who both have street credibility. A downgrade was not an option.

Of all the guys Ria pointed out, this one particular guy stood out from the rest. He was tall, dark skinned, with a fresh haircut—his name was David. David wasn't the average Peoria guy, he had a Chicago swag. I kept my eye on David and later found out that we frequented the same places. When I would go to functions, the anticipation of him being there was implacable.

David approached me one weekend at the park where everyone would come and hang out. He and Ria knew each other from high school so when he caught sight of her he greeted her.

"Hey Ria, how's it been?" he asked.

"Great," Ria responded as she smiled and shook her head. Ria, knew I liked David so this was the perfect opportunity to make an introduction. He looked me up and down and smirked.

"Ria, introduce me to your friend," he said.

I stuck out my hand and introduced myself. "Hi. My name is Alecia, how are you?"

"Wonderful now," he said with a smile on his face.

"Yeah, I've seen you around,".

"Oh so you noticed me then, huh?" he asked as he stepped closer to me. My face lit up and my entire body shivered with goosebumps. He leaned in and whispered in my ear "It ain't trick-in if you got it." When he pulled back he took my hand and passed me his phone number with a smile on his face.

I was unsure by what he meant but it sounded sexy. Since he was older, I assumed it was a "snatch her up line". Ria sensing my confusion clarified and rephrased his words.

"Girl what he said was, I want to give you some money for a little bit of your time," she explained.

"What?" I replied shocked. "Hell naw," Ria and I both looked at one another and started laughing. I couldn't believe it. Finally, the opportunity was offered to me to be with another man, yet all I could think about was, 'What if

Terrance finds out?' I went back and forth in my mind, but I knew I didn't want to pass this up. For David, this was a chance I was willing to take. Men keep a side piece all the time, why couldn't I? After all the bull crap Terrance put me through, my decision to give David a chance wasn't hard to make.

It was time for payback.

***

It was that time again for the Circle City Classic in Indianapolis, Indiana, For two years Ria and I made this our traditional girls trip. There was always great entertainment, great food, and sexy men. We would have a good dinner and the guys were always dessert—well, only the ones with the most swag and money. Ria and I had our rooms booked and our bags packed and ready the week before. The classic brought guys from all the surroundings areas—Chicago, St. Louis and even Detroit—men with money ready to blow it with little cuties like myself. For the ladies, attire was all that mattered especially when it came time to hit up the clubs. You had to have the right fit for the right guy, and I made sure to come with my A game.

Terrance and I had been spending more time apart. Although we still lived together, quality time was no longer priority. Terrance was constantly carrying on with other females which eventually left me with no choice except to slide off and do me.

A while had passed since David gave me his number, but I still kept it tucked away for "just in case" moments like these. As I paced back and forth I finally decided to use it.

"Hello," David answered.

"Hey, how are you?"

"Who's this," David asked

" Alecia…."

My heart pounded harder and grew heavier. I wasn't sure if he was still interested or even if I had the right number. Right when I was about to hang up he said,

"What's up little sexy!"

Within minutes the conversation went from 0 to 100.

"So let's hook up this week," David suggested.

"Okay," I responded with no hesitation. I didn't want to come off easy, but he had a way with words. However, we had one problem—he had a woman and I had a man; craving each other we knew there was only one option.

"Where and when?" I asked, excited that we were actually doing this.

"Thursday," he confirmed, "I'll text you the info."

As soon as I hung the phone up, I called Ria.

"Girl you would never believe who I just got off the phone with."

"Who?" Ria asked

"DAVID," I shouted, " *and* we hooking up this weekend."

Ria and I had it out for the same type of guys. The type of guys who knew what to do with their money, in other words guys who would "empty out those pockets." Whenever it came to this type of action, Ria was my go-to home girl.

"I'm not mad at you, shit get that money," Ria replied in excitement.

I knew I would go through with it ;yet, there were two things on my mind. First, where would I tell Terrance I'm going? Second I was hoping not to see anyone he knew at the hotel. It's funny because I've been loyal to him throughout our entire relationship, but the feeling of stepping out on him kept picking at me. I shook it off and eventually pulled myself together. No longer questioning it I decided I was ready to creep off with David.

***

Thursday came fast. I was nervous yet excited for the date. I didn't know what to expect; yet, what I did know was that I wanted to have cute a two-piece lingerie set and I knew exactly where to get it—my favorite shop *Victoria's*. I could never go wrong with a red lace bra and matching panties. I needed something that would entice David because I planned on getting as much money as possible out of him.

As the day went on Terrance had a full schedule of errands to run, so coming up with some elaborate story was unnecessary. Instead, I waited patiently for David to contact me. It was about 5:30pm when my phone finally went off,

"Hello," I answered.

"Hey gorgeous. How are you this is David."

"One second," I replied as I stepped out my apartment. Terrance was in the next room watching television and I didn't want him to hear our conversation. David and I had to be very careful. "Hello, I'm back how are you?"

"Great," David replied. "I was just confirming what time I'll be expecting you. How does 7:30pm sound with you?"

"That sounds great," I responded.

"Okay, cool. Meet me at the Pere room 217." We exchanged a few words before hanging up. The excitement I felt was unimaginable. I've had my eye on David for a long time and it was finally happening. I knew it was going to be an on interesting evening. My bag was packed and hidden in my trunk under my spare tire, I had packed an extra pair of panties and some personal hygiene items. I was fully prepared. Nervous as ever, I took a deep breath and said to myself "Get that money". I got myself together and left out the house.

As I was headed downtown towards the hotel one of my favorite songs came on the radio "T-shirt with my panties on" by Adina Howard. It was as if the radio station knew exactly where I was headed.

When I pulled up to the hotel, I looked in the mirror to apply a little lip-gloss and brushed my hair back. After checking myself out and making sure I looked flawless, I was ready to go inside. As I took the elevator to the second floor my stomach felt like it was in my back. My nerves were getting the best of me but there was no turning back now. I softly knocked and the door opened slowly. I wasn't able to see David's face because he was standing behind the door as I walked in.

"Hey come in. Sit down and make yourself comfortable. Would you like a drink?" He offered.

"Yes, why not," I responded. The room was foggy from weed smoke, yet I didn't mind. I thought maybe the contact would help relax me. As I walked into the room I noticed the beautiful artwork on the wall. There was one painting with a guy pouring wine into a woman's mouth as she laid nude on the bed in rose petals. That was about the sexiest painting I've ever seen in my entire life, the room just had sexuality written all over it.

"Do you smoke?" David asked

"No," I responded. However, I wanted to loosen up so I took a few puffs. I needed to be in a place where I felt ready for whatever and David knew exactly what it would take to spark my match.

David took my face by his hands and kissed me. He laid me on the bed while he caressed my body from top to bottom. The feeling was unimaginable and the intensity of the room caused my head to go around in circles. David stroked his dark chocolate Mandingo and found his way inside of me. His girth touched every crevice of my walls and I clawed into his back moaning in sweet pleasure. The tighter I gripped, the stronger his thrust. Our bodies rocked in unison and the sound of our breathing became out soundtrack. My walls pulsated releasing the flooded river inside me forcing David to open his gates and pour into me. It was , perfect.

We lay in the bed for about an hour and neither one of us said a word. My body was stiff and the only movement I had were my eyes looking over at the clock to check the time. "Oh shit it's time to go," I said to myself. I jumped out of bed to take a shower. As I got dressed David just stood there and stared.

"Did you enjoy yourself?" he asked with a smirk across his face.

"Most definitely," I replied I was worried about Terrance calling my phone so I needed to get moving fast. As I was leaving David handed me an envelope and thanked me for coming.

I quickly headed out the hotel to get in my car replaying the crazy events that just took place. As I was driving home I wondered what was inside the envelope. I mean, I knew it was money but I was curious as to how much. Finally, I pulled over, opened it up, and began counting. Ten, twenty, one hundred, three hundred, five hundred dollars. "FIVE

HUNDRED DOLLARS!" I screamed. I was elated and just had to share the new with Ria.

"Girl, girl, girl! I just left the room with David trickin' ass" I said.

"What happened?" she asked anxious to hear the story.

"Five hundred dollars is what happened," I shouted into the phone. We both laughed so hard.

"Get you some rest, crazy" Ria said, "We leave tomorrow for the Circle City Classic."

***

Tomorrow came fast and it was time for us to ride out. My pocket book was loaded with money and I was ready to take Indianapolis over. Terrance didn't mind me gone for the weekend since he always had something to do in Chicago. At 9:30am Ria picked me up. I gave Terrance a peck on the lips and headed out. Terrance could tell the change in my behavior. I no longer cooked for him—not breakfast, lunch, or dinner. I ignored him and showed no interest yet he never confronted me about it. Even if he did, it wouldn't make a difference. This was the new Alecia and I didn't care who didn't like it.

Ria and I were ready and headed to Indianapolis. When we pulled up to check into the Hyatt Regency, there were nothing but exotic cars parked outside the hotel. At check in we noticed a few familiar faces from Chicago. Seeing them I knew we would all link up. Moments later, David walked in. He was dressed to impress and dripped with iced out jewelry. I looked his way and smiled hoping to catch his attention, however he walked right pass me with his woman a few feet behind. Seeing the expression on my face Ria checked me.

"You cannot be mad at him Alecia. You have a man." I knew she was right. I gave it some thought and decided to get over it. I wouldn't let this little mishap ruin our weekend. We linked up with two of our male friends and took the town over. At every club we attended, we went in VIP status. We popped bottles all weekend—Moet, Don Perion, Ace of Spades—you name it, the guys made sure we had it. When we weren't clubbing we were shopping. We felt like Boss's and we operated as such. No one could tell us anything. After a long weekend of festivities, it was time to head back home. As we were on the highway heading back home, I noticed I hadn't heard from Terrance the entire weekend. The thought of this troubled me. I knew what Terrance was capable of when I was out of sight and out of mind. Something was up. Ria must have been reading my mind.

"Have you heard from your boo?" She asked.

"Nope, not one time," I replied. Ria's face frowned then she took a deep breath.

"I wanted to tell you something, but wanted to wait until after our trip," she started. "I saw Terrance at the liquor store last weekend with some chic. I didn't think you would care that much especially since you had hooked up with David, but FYI."

I sat still and quiet taking everything in she had said. This was it. It was time for Terrance and me to go separate ways. We were both doing our own thing and the respect was no longer there.

"You know what Ria, you're right. I don't even care anymore. I'm about to do me!"

4

THE BREAK UP

I was approaching my 20th birthday and was very excited. My arm was doing fine and the motor skills in my fingers were coming back. I just bought a new car and remodeled my apartment for a new look. Only thing old was Terrance.

At twenty-years-old, I was making moves, surrounding myself around people with money or class. I was always the youngest of them all but that hardly ever mattered because I stayed laid back and out the way.

My brother was at the top of his game and with all the money that was being made Steve always made sure to spoil me with lavish gifts.

Ring, ring.

"Hello," I answered.

"What's up little sis. Happy birthday."

"Aww, thank you," I replied.

"Are you home?" Steve asked.

" Yes, I'm home."

"Okay, sounds good. I'm heading over now to bring you your birthday gift."

"Okay Steve, see you in a few."

I was very excited to see what Steve had bought me, especially since he always went out his way for me. I went on to get my clothes ready for later on that evening, Steve had put together a birthday party for me in my hometown at Club E and even though I wasn't quite legal yet to be in the club, the owner and I was cool so he gave me a pass.

Knock, knock.

"Who is it?" I asked

"Steve, open the door Alecia." I unlocked the doors letting him come in.

"Wow, that was fast you getting over here."

"I told you I was close. Now turn around short stuff, and close your eyes." I did as I was told, eager to know what my gift was. "Okay, you can open them now."

"OH MY GOD. A LOUIS BAG," I squealed. In front of me was a Louis Vuitton clutch bag, in the colors beige and brown. It was the exclusive one I had seen on Michigan Ave. a few months ago in Chicago, I had showed Steve a picture of it sometime ago but didn't think nothing of it or that he would even spend that much money on a bag for me.

"Aww, thank you so much brother, you're the best," I said with tears rolling down my cheeks.

"No problem," he said then hugged me. We both just smiled. "Ok, I gotta run sis. have a few errands to make before your party tonight so I'll see you then. Love ya."

I gave Steve another hug and locked the door behind him. I turned around to go back to admiring my new bag and noticed Terrance was still sitting on the couch watching TV. Terrance had not said a word the entire time Steve was over, to the point I almost forgot he was there. Steve and Terrance never got along. Whenever Steve would come over to the house to visit, he ignored Terrance. It seemed I was starting to do the same. I grabbed my new bag and went into the bedroom gawking at its beauty. A few minutes later, I heard footsteps coming towards the room.

"Hey baby, Happy Birthday," Terrance said then handed me a white box with a big red bow on top. I wasn't impressed with his gestured but I figured I would be nice. It's the thought that counts, right? I took the box from Terrance, and slowly removed the bow while lifting the box cover. Inside, I ripped off the tissue paper that stood between me and gift. Once unraveled, I was very pleased with the gift. It was a beautiful and very expensive Fendi Canvas leather Bag. To be honest, I absolutely loved the bag, but I was over all the material gifts from Terrance. I was ready to move on.

***

My party was in Peoria at Club E and it was packed. I was excited to see everyone and even hoped that David would show up. Despite our incident in Indianapolis at the Circle City Classic, he still had my undivided attention whenever I would see him.

After a few hours, David finally came walking into the club wearing a Coogie Sweat Suit. With his swag, David could attract attention from miles away; everyone around him showed him love. That was the shit that turned me on about him. He would step into the club and the DJ instantly gave him a shout out. It was a respect factor; David was well known in the city. In a packed room, he spotted me out and swiftly came up behind me. Discreetly, he gave me a kiss on my cheek and a hand full of money. This life was designed for me to receive and take at any cost and I did just that with him and all these men.

Enjoying my night, I didn't notice Terrance sitting back watching my every move that night. He stayed quiet yet his eyes screamed with rage. I could feel the tension in the air coming off him and I knew he must have saw David. Shortly after David walked away, Terrance walked up to me and head butted me. This took me by surprise and I didn't know what to do. When I got myself in order, he leaned in and hissed "Let's go".

Terrance was pissed; I could see it in his face. He had a demonic expression and I knew I was no longer dealing with just Terrance. From the other side of the club Steve could see what was going on. He came over and asked if I was okay. Not wanting any more issues, yet still in a daze I simply replied "Yes."

As we headed home, I knew what was coming. When we walked through the door, Terrance walked in behind me and grabbed me by my neck. Before I could yell stop, his fist met my face and he pounded my face over and over again. I was so intoxicated that the blunt force against my face did not faze me, but I screamed and yelled for him to stop. He didn't care, so I forced myself to get away. I was able to get away from him to run out the door but he grabbed a hold of me and kept repeating "I'll kill you bitch". I tried to get away once again but with no success. He pushed me into the car and drove us off.

I was terrified. This was the first time I saw him carry on in this matter. We would fight all the time but never to this degree.

"Why are you doing this?" I asked him with fear in my voice.

"You stupid bitch! You stupid bitch. You've disrespected me one too many times!" Terrance shouted. He kept repeating this in a bout of fury that could not be controlled. Terrance turned off the local traffic on to the highway headed north. He was driving erratically, and all I could think to myself was the last words he said to me "I'm going to kill you." I didn't know if he was serious but sitting in the car while driving I knew he meant it.

We were about 45 minutes away from Peoria, and I begged and pleaded for him to take me back home. He ignored my cries and continued to drive. I tried to say and do anything to get him to stop, yet the more I talked, the more agitated he became. Suddenly he pulled over and grabbed me out the car. *What in the hell was he about to do to me?* I thought as I pushed away from him. He dragged me towards the back of the car and popped the trunk.

"NO, NO, NO," I yelled and pleaded. But he did not listen. He took me by my legs and threw me into the trunk. It was pitch dark outside with hardly any cars on the highway. He slammed the trunk on top of me and I knew he was serious. Terrance was going to kill me.

No one could see me or hear my voice. I was in the trunk and all I could hear were the tire marks as he pulled off.

"TERRANCE!" I screamed over and over. "STOP THE CAR. PLEASE STOP THE CAR."

I couldn't breathe yet I didn't know what else to do. I continued to kick and yelled desperately hoping for Terrance to pull over. I could feel the car swerving from side to side. Terrance was not only erratic; he was also drunk. I was convinced if Terrance didn't kill me, a car accident would. Scared and exhausted, I did the only thing I thought would work. I prayed. I asked God to forgive me for my sins and to help me during this time. There was so much fear within my heart. I didn't know what was going through Terrance's head and I wasn't sure I wanted to find out.

About an hour had passed since we were on the highway

before Terrance finally pulled the car over. My chest tightened, my face was drenched with sweat, and my heart was racing with fear. After a few seconds, I could hear the trunk lock open. I gasped for breath while coughing and trying to catch my breath.

"Alecia, get out and drive," he yelled. I was scared to climb out the trunk, but I knew I had no choice. Without hesitation, I quickly stepped out. I must not have moved fast enough because he then tightly grabbed me by the back of my neck.

"Terrance, you're hurting me," I said.

"Shut up, bitch," Terrance responded. "Get in the car and drive," he said as he pushed me away from him. I moved quickly towards the driver's door. With Terrance behind me, I knew this could be my only chance. I quickly got into the car and locked all the doors. He was not going to get in. Terrance came to the car pulling at all the doors.

"Open the fucking door Alecia," he shouted angrily.

Without saying a word, I pulled off and left him on the highway. I made a U-turn to head south and try to get home. As I looked across the interstate, I saw Terrance on the other side of the highway jumping and shouting. I was sure he was calling me all types of names, but this time he was the bitch ass who was left on the highway stranded. I was proud of myself for moving as fast. I can't believe this man had the audacity to put me in the back of *my* trunk. He kidnapped me! The shit was unreal. I looked into the rearview mirror saddened by my reflection. Just hours ago I was celebrating my birthday having the best time of my life. And now my face was dirty and sweaty from all the makeup and tears I cried. In the rearview, I saw Terrance still jumping up and down.

My heart began to ache with guilt. *Maybe this was my fault.* If I would of done right by my man none of this would have happened, I thought. The guilt was unbearable. All I could do was think of what would happen to him. How could I ever live with knowing I left him on the highway? I was about five miles away but I couldn't take it. I turned back around to get him. Once I reached him, I pulled over and waited, watching Terrance walk up the road towards the car. He looked delusional and exhausted. A part of me felt bad for him. When Terrance reached the car, he got in, laid his seat back, and fell asleep.

***

The next morning we said nothing to each other. There was no way I was speaking to him for what he had put me through the night before. As I began to get ready for work, I felt Terrance behind me.

"Alecia."

"Yes, Terrance?" I responded with an attitude.

"I'm truly sorry, Alecia… for my actions last night." I turned around and looked at him with a disgrace. Without responding to his sorry excuse of an apology, I walked past him towards the bathroom. It was better to stay silent and avoid further confrontation then engage him and his foolishness. I continued to ignore him and got ready for work.

My day at work was short. I made plans with Ria to hang out after work and get drinks at a small club that just opened called *Club Illi*. The owner, William, was cool as hell. Club *Illi* was the go-to spot after work due to their amazing happy hour specials. William would always flirt with me when I came into his club, but I knew he was a ladies' man—all the women were crazy about him. Entertaining him was not in my game plan. I had a good reputation in the streets; I wasn't going to destroy my character by sleeping around.

The idea of having drinks for happy hour was well overdue. As soon as Ria and I walked into the club, William came straight over and greeted us. We were always VIP, so he always had us set up and ready. Every night after he closed the club, William would have gatherings at his house. Those who were invited would go over to smoke or play cards and hang out. Although he often invited me, I would never go because to me it seemed like some booty call. That night William tried so hard to convince me to come by, but I was not interested. As we were heading out, Ria mentioned she wanted to go. After some pleading, I agreed, and we headed to William's house.

When we arrived, we walked right in. William's house was extravagant. Even from the outside, it seemed it didn't belong in the neighborhood. His house was located on the South side of Peoria where many of the houses were old and run down; however, his home seemed like it never aged. This was all the more reason I was impressed with William—he always kept you wondering what else he had up his sleeves. Inside, chandeliers hung from the ceiling and mirrors decorated the walls. I even saw a Jacuzzi. Williams place was a bachelor pad. We walked past the entrance and notice William across the room entertaining other guests. I saw his face light up when he noticed that we showed up. He excused himself from his guest and approached me.

"I'm glad you changed your mind. Let me show you around," William said when he reached me.

I gave him a look warning him to not try it, but he was a

gentleman. We hung out in his bedroom and talked for a while. I didn't have much to say but that didn't stop him from talking to me. I thought it was funny how we continued our conversation as if we knew one another personally. I was intrigued. He was much older and knew how to keep my attention. At the end of the night William and I exchanged numbers. It would only be the beginning.

***

The next day I woke up in bed with an aching hangover. *Too many damn drinks,* I said to myself. I rolled over to an empty side and saw that Terrance never made it home. I rolled my eyes and rolled back over. Since that last episode, I could care less about him being here. Before I could fall asleep my phone rang.

"Hello," I answered.

"Good morning beautiful," the deep voice greeted. I smiled already knowing who it was.

"Good Morning," I said.

I knew William was a ladies' man and I could see why. He was so charming. Whatever he was selling, I was buying. William wanted to move fast; I wanted to take things easy. With so much going on I didn't want the extra bullshit in my life; however, William made things feel ok. He was different and chill, that's what I liked about him the most. He always kept a smile on my face. *How could I deny that?*

"How are you, Ms. Alecia?" William asked. I laughed to myself, impressed by him referring to me as 'Ms.' It made me feel like a grown woman.

"I'm great and you?" I responded.

"Good. So, look. I was thinking you can stop by the

club tonight; maybe we can sit, talk, and entertain each other," he said.

"Entertain?" I responded. "what do you mean, 'entertain'?"

"Oh no, not like that. Just a little music, darts or even pool, and of course I have your favorite drink."

"Oh you do?" I said while playfully twirling my hair. "And what is that?"

"Vodka and cranberry, correct?" I smiled. I guess he does pay attention.

"Yes that's right. Ok, sounds like a plan." We talked a little more than ended the call.

Later that night, I arrived at the club anxious to see William. The club was quiet, hardly anyone came by. I knew that he had it all planned but I just went along with it. The atmosphere was relaxing so I didn't complain. We stayed until closing and as I was getting ready to go he came over to me.

"So, would you like to stop by the house, maybe for a movie?", he asked, in a deep tone voice that gave me chills all over my body. *This was a setup*, I thought. He knew he would get me to agree since the mood was right. What was worse was his sex appeal made me go crazy

"Yea, I'll stop by. Why not," I responded.

I was anxious the entire ride to William's house. All I could do was think what I was getting myself into. When we arrived, the soft fragrance of lilac enveloped us. It was cozy and romantic and quickly put me in the mood. Then I knew there was going to be trouble.

Back at his house, we sat in the living room and tried to watch a movie. I say try because he couldn't keep his hands off me.

"William, what are you doing?" I asked. He smiled but didn't stop. His massaged through my hair his lips traced my neck. The temperature in the room seemed warm up I was sure he had the heat on. "William," I moaned.

Ignoring my weak attempt to stop, he picked me up throwing me over his shoulder. His big arms around my body turned me on. He knew as much as I did. I wanted him. He carried me to his bedroom and threw me onto his King sized waterbed. My reflection in the mirror confirmed how sexy I was. Of course he couldn't keep his hands off me. He climbed on top and eagerly started to tear my clothes off as he kissed me and rubbed my breast. His hands was strong and his aggression turned me on. He was wild and fun and horny. There was an animal inside of him waiting to be unleashed. He pulled off my pants in one quick motion and grabbed the oil that was on his nightstand. He began biting on my legs as he poured oil in between my breast and rubbed it in. The sensation was overwhelming. He then put on a condom and went deep inside of me with my legs swaddling in the air. The soft touch from the silk sheets on my body and the tension inside of me from William penetration was exhilarating. This was perfect. The night was phenomenal and William and I laid in the waterbed gasping for breath satisfied from the orgasm we both experienced.

***

The year was moving fast and I had made a comeback since the motorcycle accident. Terrance and I were still 'dating' but our arrangement was more like roommates. I knew our relationship was coming to an end, which made it easier to continue relations with William.

Terrance had a lot of dealings with different guys in the streets although I was never aware exactly who. My hometown is small. Everyone knows everyone and just when you think you're getting away with something you soon find out you're just getting by. I knew first hand this truth as this was how Terrance always got caught cheating. One day my morning was starting off just right. I had some errands to run and needed to stop by William's house to pick up some money.

William was nice and would let me hold a few dollars from time to time. When I pulled up to his house there were about three cars parked outside other than William's. This was unusual considering it was early in the morning, however, I didn't think anything of it. The plan was to be in and out. I walked to his door and as soon as I walked in, Terrance walked out. My face was flushed. It was about to be trouble.

"What the hell are you doing over here, Alecia?" Terrance asked. I was speechless. How in the world was I going to get out of this one?

"Mmmmm, just to talk real quick. What's up?" I said nonchalantly. This was the only thing I could think of. I had no clue what Terrance would do. Surprisingly, he just looked at me, shook his head, and walked off.

Hearing the commotion, William came outside. He knew I dated Terrance and must have known there was trouble.

"Alecia, everything alright?" William asked.

"Hell no! Does everything look alright?" I yelled. "Damn William, why didn't you call and warn me to wait?"

"Alecia, I swear I totally forgot. I'm sorry," William said.

"SORRY? You think sorry is going to do anything?" I yelled. He just stared. "What the hell William? Now I have to go and straighten things out with Terrance," I said as I stormed back to my car. "Dam, dam, dam!" I yelled slamming my driver's door shut.

I started to head home unable to focus. I knew I need to come up with a better story other than the one I told earlier today. Terrance was going to want answers immediately as I stepped foot in the house.

When I pulled up to our home, Terrance was sitting in the car with his buddy. His face was red so I knew he was angry. I was nervous and hoped he would let me explain. When I saw his friend, my guard went down. He wouldn't put his hand on me in broad daylight. As I parked, Terrance got out the car. When I got out the car, I started to speak but was quickly interrupted when Terrance slammed my face into the window.

Boom. Boom. boom. The sound of my head banging against the window deafened me. With all his rage, Terrance repeatedly threw my head into the window of the car .

"STOP," I screamed over and over. I tried to push him off me but he was much stronger.

"Is, this the shit you want me to do to you Alecia?" he yelled, continuously pounding my head into the glass.

"STOP. TERRANCE STOP!" I cried desperately wanting help. His friend never interceded. Instead, he stood there as an accompanying bystander. My shirt was torn and my shoes came off from all the blows. The taste of blood overpowered me. All I saw was red. My face was a bloody mess. When Terrance friend saw this he finally pulled Terrance off.

"I'm telling my brother," I yelled. I never wanted to involve Steve into our mess because deep down in my heart I always knew I would go back to Terrance. This time was different. Enough was enough.

Covered in blood I ran into my house to call Steve. I wanted Terrance out my life for good. Although I loved him, I could no longer take the abuse

"Hello"? Steve answered.

"Steve help. Please help me. I can't hardly see. Terrance bust my face open," I said to Steve.

"What?" Steve shouted on the other end of the phone. He was pissed. "He did what?"

"Help me, Steve," I begged.

"Where you at, Alecia?"

"I'm at home," I responded.

"I'm on my way, sis. Stop crying. I'm on my way." With that he hung up and I knew it wouldn't take him long to get here. I could hear the rage in Steve's voice. He was upset and ready for a fight.

Steve pulled up about ten minutes later. Terrance was waiting outside. He was also for whatever was going to happen.

"What's up, Terrance let me holla at you," Steve said walking towards Terrance with his gun exposed in his pocket.

"What you want to do?" Terrance barked back. "Didn't I tell you to stay out me and your sister's business?"

"My sister is my business," Steve said reaching for his gun and pointing it at Terrance.

"NO! Steve STOP," I repeatedly yelled as bloody tears drenched my face."

"Alecia, make a decision now before someone gets hurt. I'm not playing any more games with this man." Seeing how serious Steve was I knew I had to make a decision. I looked at Terrance and sheepishly asked him to remove his belongings from the apartment.

As much as Terrance hurt me, it hurt me just as bad to

say those words. I was to blame for what just happened…at least that's how I felt. I always made myself feel responsible for him putting his hands on me and this time was no different. We had been to hell and back over the years, yet despite our issues I loved him. It ached my heart to know that the love we once had was replaced with tears and pain; yet, my heart would not let him go. It seemed Terrance and I were finally coming to an end.

***

It was now fall of 2003 and schools were back in session. The homecomings of the colleges around my hometown were always fun with a variety of entertainment, especially Southern University of Carbondale. Attending college was always a dream that never came true so to make up for it I enjoyed the college culture. David and I reconnected and he invited me to Southern University tailgate and football game. I was always down for a trip so I agreed and we made plans. I was excited to get away from everything I had gone through months prior with Terrance. A few months had passed since I kicked him out my apartment. I missed him but the image of his hands banging into my face constantly replayed in my head. I needed to clear my mind and this trip was what I needed. When we arrived at the college we recognized many people from our hometown, many of which knew the both of us. Not wanting to get caught we often had to play as if we were not together. This became tiring and the trip wasn't what I thought it would be. In fact, it was out right boring. So much time passed since we last connected we no longer had anything to talk about. All I wanted was some money and for David to take me home. Later that evening David and I went back to the room to relax and eat dinner. My body was calling for a shower from all the heat it had to be 100 degrees outside. As I got undressed to get into the shower David came into the bathroom making sexual eye contact but I wasn't enthusiastic at all and he could tell.

"Alecia, are you okay baby?" he asked.

"Yes, just a little tired." He looked at me inquisitively, trying to decipher whether or not I was telling the truth. I wasn't tired. The truth was , I just couldn't get into the vibe of being alone with him. For me this was business. I stepped out the shower to dry off while David walked out the bathroom. As I was drying off my phone rang,

"Hello," I answered.

"Hey Alecia, this is Ria. I just heard Terrance and two chic's were pulled over on the highway and taken into custody by the authorities."

"What? Are you serious? Oh my God I can't believe this," I shouted into the phone. My hands started to shake uncontrollably. An instant headache came over me. I was speechless.

"Alecia, Alecia," I heard Ria say. "Are you there?"

"Yes, yes I'm here," I said as my voice trembled. " I'll talk with you later."

My entire body became numb and weak. I felt as if my whole life had been shattered. I thought this was what I wanted—Terrance out my life. I did, but not this way. Not with him going to jail. I no longer wanted to be with him, but I still loved him and wanted everything to be okay. I stood there in a daze with my phone in my hand. *How could this be happening?*

"Alecia, baby, Alecia, what's going on?" David asked.

"No, everything is not okay," I replied. "I have an

emergency back home we must leave now."

***

I quickly packed my bags and made David take me back to Peoria. Carbondale University was about five hours away from Peoria so the drive back home was anxiety driven; all I could do was worry myself to pieces. As we headed back to Peoria, David tried to do everything in his power to make the ride comfortable. He didn't speak much and made sure to keep the music low. It was quiet, too quiet. Even though David and I never got personal, right then and there, I needed to talk. The pain was too much to keep silent.

"David," I said. He shifted his gaze toward me then back on the road lowering the music, letting me know he was listening. I continued, "My guy just got taken into custody by the authorities. I don't know what's going on but I'm sure it's not good."

"Why would you think that?" he asked, not taking his eyes off the road.

" Let's just say I know of what he's involved in." David nodded his head. I knew that was enough for him to understand what I meant. "I really don't know how to feel right now."

"What do you mean Alecia?" I shifted in my seat. As much as I needed to talk, I couldn't help to feel a little weird having this conversation with him. I took a deep breath and let it all out.

"Well, we've been separated for the past few months. We still speak but we no longer live together. Well…I made him get out. He's been physical abusing me."

"WHAT! Fighting you Alecia?" David said surprised by

my confession. "Alecia you don't deserve that. I'm so sorry to hear this." He then reached over and grabbed my hand slightly squeezing it. I feel tears beginning to well up in my eyes. This was the first time I said out loud that I was abused by Terrance; yet, now I was desperate to know if he was ok. I was so conflicted and my feelings didn't make sense, yet I could not stop them from flowing.

"Look Alecia, do what your heart tells you. I don't want to get into your personal business but I will say this, do what's best for you." I nodded.

"Thank you, David...thanks for listening."

It was about 2 AM when David and I pulled into Peoria. I was happy to finally be home, but I needed to get back in town to find out about Terrance's legal issues. David dropped me off at my car and I started to head home. When I was just a few minutes away from home my phone rang.

"Hello," I answered and the familiar voice replied. "Terrane, what happened Terrance?" I asked eagerly wanting to make sense of everything. My questions was met with a surge of apologies.

"Alecia, listen baby... it's over, it's all over," he said on the other end of the receiver.

"What's over Terrance? Stop talking that way, you're scaring me," I said while trying to keep my eyes on the road.

"Alecia, I was caught red-handed baby, I messed up this time." I knew what he meant but I didn't want to believe it. My vision started to blur and I could taste the salty droplets that streamed down my face. I quickly pulled into my driveway.

"Terrance, we can get a lawyer everything will be okay, won't it?"

"No Alecia, I'm afraid not. not this time." How could

this have happened. I was flooded with emotions and couldn't wrap my head around what to feel. Time stood still. Terrance was going away for good. "Look here Alecia, I'm sorry for putting my hands on you and cheating. You deserve better—a real man—not a coward like myself."

We both cried. This was goodbye. The game finally caught up to him which meant it also caught up with me. Terrence always gave me the best of everything when it came to material needs, now that he was gone, those gifts would stop.

"I'm facing five to seven years, Alecia. "I do understand if you move on since we weren't in a good place," he said. "You deserve better," he repeated.

For a moment, I stayed quiet, not exactly sure what to say or where to start. What do you say to a person you love that has hurt you the most? It just didn't make sense but I knew silence wasn't the answer.

"I love you Terrance. I'm sorry for a lot of my wrongdoing as well. I haven't been an angel in this relationship either, but I didn't deserve a lot of what you did to me. You took a piece of me that nearly broke me down. You made me suffer in so many ways. Do you know how many sleepless nights I had waiting for you to come home, do you? You almost killed me," I said as I felt anger begin to stir. I took a deep breath and continued. "Terrance we took a long ride together, but it has come to an end. Despite it all, I want you to know I will always love you Terrance."

"I will too, Alecia. Take care of yourself baby and be strong. Remember what I taught you—be an independent woman, you already are."

Click.

That was the last time we spoke to each other. Terrance

and I were officially over.

5
THE STAGE
2004

A new year meant new people and new endeavors. What it also meant was I was finally turning twenty-one. This was a big relief because I no longer needed other female's ID's to get into the club. I hated that. In a couple of months, I no longer had to worry about that.

This year also came with a new relationship. Terrance was no longer in the picture, and I ended things with both David and William. The old needed to stay with the old. I was now with Lamar and things were going great. After a few months of dating I moved him into my apartment. He was staying in Peoria for a few months so it just made sense to me. Lamar was a student at Morehouse College in Atlanta, a city I loved so much. Atlanta was filled with lots of opportunity and had some of the best colleges. I aspired to go back to college for a degree in Pharmacy and Lamar's ambition inspired me consider my future. Life with Lamar was different from what I was used to. We would talk a lot about life goals and discuss our five year goals. This was something I never thought about because I was infatuated with the here and now. The lifestyle I was used too was only about material pleasures and great sex. Although I had a job, my future wasn't something that interested me enough to discuss.

One weekend, we were at home doing some cleaning. I was in the kitchen when Lamar walked in.

"Hey Alecia, are we still going dancing at the Lounge this evening?"

"Yes indeed," I replied with a huge smile on my face. Lamar didn't have much money—something I wasn't used to—but he was very respectful and that was something I hadn't been accustomed to in a long time. As I continued to wash the dishes he put his arm around my waist.

"Alecia, I want to have a conversation with you," he said gently turning me around and we face each other. He looked me in my eye and said, " I want you to relocate. Move to Atlanta with me."

"Huh? Atlanta!" I said surprisingly. *Is he crazy?*

"Yes Alecia, Atlanta. What you think about moving there with me?"

It had only been four months since we've dated so, I was unsure if I was ready for that big of a move. Moving would mean so many changes. Changes that I wasn't sure I was ready to experience.

"Lamar, give me some time to decide," I said as I dried my hands. " After these dishes, I'm going to head out to the mall. I'll be back shortly."

I went to the mall and stopped at my favorite store, Famous Barr.—they were the only store in town that carried my favorite fashion line, *Dereon*. While shopping, I bumped into an old friend who I haven't seen in years.

"Hey Secret, how are you?" I greeted.

"I'm good, girl, life is great as you can see," as she showed off her designer bag and blinged out jewels.

"Yes girl! You have that money glow to you," I said while laughing.

"Girl, yes. You know I'm all about getting some money," she said as we both laughed. "By the way how you been?" Secret asked.

"I'm good. Just working and dating. You know, living life."

I could tell Secret had a major source of income from the amount of purchases she had made. She was holding about ten shopping bags. I didn't want to be nosey but I couldn't help but ask where she worked. How could she afford all this.

"Where do you work now Secret?" I asked.

"The Bullet Gentleman's Club," she responded.

"What's that?"

"A strip club," she said confidently. My eyes grew big. *A strip club?* I couldn't believe it. Secret was a stripper. As shocking as this was, it sparked my curiosity. A stripper was an interesting job and since I was considering the move, I knew I needed extra money and I needed it quick.

"Hey, check it out Secret, I'm in the process of moving and could used some extra cash. I want to dance too."

"Are you serious?" Secret asked. Surprised by my inquiry she broke out in laughter. She looked at me and noticed my facial expression. "Oh, you are serious."

"Yes, I'm dead serious," I said.

"Well, auditions are held on Tuesdays. You'll need a pair of high heels and a sexy dress," Secret said.

"Sounds good, talk to you then." We exchanged

numbers then went our separate ways.

I went to the cashier to complete my purchase. As I paid the cashier, I replayed the conversation I had and couldn't believe had just taken place. Money was the only thing on my mind and as I walked out the mall to get into my car I couldn't believe what I just agreed to. The idea of taking my clothes off for strangers did not sit well with me. I know I dealt with guys in the past that did nice things for me, but this was different. How would I explain this to Lamar? We just started dating. What would he think if I told him I wanted to be a stripper? There were so many thoughts running through my head; yet, the idea of all the money I could make trumped all my worries. Money was all that mattered.

When I made it home Lamar was in the shower getting ready for our date later that evening. I paced back and forth through the apartment and waited until he got out the shower to discuss what I was thinking. When I heard the water cut off, I nervously I started biting my nails. After what seemed like ages, Lamar walked into the living room.

"What's wrong Alecia? you keep moving around." The look I gave him let him know that something crazy about to come out my mouth. He took a deep breath and sat down. "Whatever it is Alecia, just say it now please."

"Look Lamar, I have an opportunity to make a whole lot of money before we move to Atlanta, but..." I trailed off not wanting to say what the opportunity was.

"But what?" Lamar asked.

"I don't think you're going to like the idea," I admitted, still not wanting to share what it is. Lamar's eyebrows rose and he studied me. Not wanting to look him in his eye, I avoided his gaze.

"Dancing?" he guessed. My head shot up. How could he

possibly figure that out? "Dancing." When he put it that way, it didn't sound so bad, it sounded a little more professional. Not a stripper, a dancer.

"Yes, dancing," I confirmed.

"Where?" Lamar asked.

"At this club over in Champaign, it's about two hours away." Lamar looked at me inquisitively. I couldn't read him as he stayed quiet for a few more moments. I wanted to him to say something, anything to ease up the tension in the room, but he stayed quiet for what seemed like hours. Before I could break the silence, he spoke up.

"It's up to you Alecia. I'm cool with it, just make the right choices."

Just like that the conversation was over. That was easy. Relieved by Lamar's response, I knew I still had one more hurdle—my brother. How would I explain this to Steve? He would kill me if he knew I was doing such a thing. Steve looked to me more as his daughter than his sister. I knew if I told him this, he wouldn't approve, no matter how much money was involved.

***

Tuesday came sooner than I could imagine. I worked at the pharmacy for only half a day, that way I could prepare myself for the audition. My bag was packed and ready to go with exactly everything Secret told me to bring. When Secret picked me up anxiety brewed inside. *I was really doing this.* As I climbed into the car, Secret had a big grin across her face.

"Let's get this money," she said clearly excited I was auditioning.

"Oh yes," I replied. Secret was dressed very elegant. She

wore a black long black spaghetti strap dress that had two thigh-high splits on each side. It was sexy but classy. She looked exotic and had a sensual aura. She was so enticing that she even had me feeling some type of way looking at her. Secret proved that being sexy was all about the look and the vibe.

As we drove and talked my thoughts raced and my nerves were bad. I was always about my money but this was some new shit. The idea of a bunch of strangers looking at my naked body grossed me out. The more I thought about it the more my nerves bothered me. I needed a drink.

We pulled up a block away from the club, and stopped by the liquor store for a few drinks. Auditions were in a half hour so we had some extra time to hang out. I needed to take it to the head quick so I could loosen up. We bought a bottle of Tanqueray Vodka, then took two shots. It was just what I needed to calm my nerves. We got back in the car and continued the drive.

When we arrived at the club, we parked and touched up our make-up. Before getting out, Secret offered a few tips.

"Make sure your walk is sexy and slow. Tease the crowd, they love that and it gets you more tips. Move your hips around, touch your thighs softly, all that It's all about the vibe you give out—plus this is only a topless club," Secret said.

"That's it?" I asked shocked and relieved.

"Yes girl. You thought you were going to take it all off?" Secret laughed.

"Yes," I admitted. "I feel so much better knowing that I don't have to. Okay, I'm ready, let's go in." As we walked into the club the owner's wife, Tasha, was standing at the door.

"Are you ready to audition?" Tasha asked.

"Yes," I nervously responded.

"Okay, you have ten minutes to get ready and come to the bar." I walked away not sure where the dressing room was.

"Where's the dressing room Secret?"

"You're standing in it," she replied.

"Huh?" I asked confused by her answer. The room looked like a storage area. There were cleaning products and toiletry everywhere. I was expecting glass mirrors all over the wall with bright lights, an on-call makeup artist, and a large collection beautiful gowns and outfits to wear to walk down the runway. Instead I walked into a janitor's closet—literally.

"Get ready girl," Secret said as she walked out the dressing room. Disappointed but determined to get it over with, I pulled my clothes out my bag, I took out two black dresses that I had from some time ago. They fit tight and showed a lot of cleavage, the perfect combination for a new dancer. Once I finished getting dressed, I went on to take one more shot before heading out.

I walked over to the bar area and waited for the next direction. Moments later, Tasha approached me.

"What's your stage name?" Tasha asked.

"Stage name?" I asked confused.

"Yea, what will you like to go by?"

Secret never said anything about a stage name. I had to think fast.

"Autumn," I finally said. "Yea, I'll go with Autumn."

Tasha wrote down my name and took it to the DJ. It felt like my feet were stuck to the floor. I was frozen with anxiety yet I tried to calm my nerves thinking about all the tips Secret gave me. It wasn't long before I had to put those tips to use.

"Autumn, to the stage," the DJ announced.

As I approached the stage I took a deep breath and confidently strutted down the runway—as if I knew what I was doing. When the music started to play the liquor started to kick in.

Baby, baby, baby, I heard the music through the speakers. It was a TLC song that I enjoyed, but I forget the name. I began to loosen up and became comfortable with the atmosphere. I must have been doing a great job because guys were coming up to the stage and throwing money. The more they threw the more I danced. Quick and easy money. Before I knew it, it was over. As I stepped down off the stage, Tasha approached me.

"When would you like to start?" she asked. I couldn't believe it. I was going to be a dancer. My excitement couldn't be contained.

"Tonight, if possible," I said eagerly.

"Sounds good. Welcome to the Bullet," she said and smiled. Just like that I became a dancer.

My plan was to make $400 to $600 a night for the following three months and saving all of it. I was on a mission to make as much as money as possible before we moved to Atlanta. My mission was to hustle everyone who came through that door. It was time to get paid and I was ready.

6
A NEW CITY

Everything was going smoothly for the move. We were exactly three months away before the move to Atlanta, and I was very excited. While I danced, Lamar hustled. I didn't approve of it because he had so much to lose, yet I he still needed to carry his own weight. If this was the way, then I just let it rock. Saving meant I worked a lot. My work schedule was set; I would work doubles on Sunday and Monday at the pharmacy and Tuesday through Saturday at the Gentleman's Club. With all work, I saved all my money, so I had no time to play around. My goal was to save ten-thousand dollars by June 7th, and I only had a little under three months to make this happen. At the rate I was going, I knew it would happen if I continued to follow my plan. When the date came, it was time to pack up and head south. I saved exactly fifteen thousand dollars and was proud of it. I already signed my lease for my apartment in Atlanta, and my job with CVS had already transferred me. Everything was in place. Despite my excitement, I was sad to be leaving and moving so far away. My mommy was sad I was leaving, but I promised to come back for her, Steve and my mother's oldest sister, Wanda were responsible to make sure my mother was taking care of. Lamar had to stay behind for another month, because someone broke into my car and stole his money. It was hard leaving him behind but I was off and ready to live my best life in Atlanta and mingle a bit until he got there.

Don't get me wrong, I loved Lamar but we weren't married. This was my first official year of being legal and able to club hop and I wanted to experience it all. I was ready to meet some new faces, especially those who were able to direct me to where the cash was at.

My new apartment was beautiful but expensive. The new life came with a high-ticket cost. My rent was nine-hundred dollars—a big difference from my small apartment in Peoria. With such high rent, I knew I would have to make something shake fast. Lamar only worked part-time since he went to school full time. Although I loved it Atlanta, I knew I would need to adjust quickly to the new city.

The thought of dancing in Atlanta was terrifying, especially because the clubs were predominantly black. I was from a small club with a different layout for dancing. Atlanta clubs were nude and almost everything went down, and I mean *everything*.

Thirty minute VIP's for $150.00 includes a dance *and* blow job.

One hour VIP's for $300.00 includes a dance, blow job, *and* sex.

Dancing in Atlanta was not just dancing.

My mind couldn't even grasp the fact I had to get completely nude so I could not imagine having sex with people I didn't even know. That was crazy. The good thing was every club wasn't like that. As a newbie, you had to pay attention to what part of the city you worked in. Aside from the extra services, the biggest difference was the type of dancing. Most clubs involved dancers shaking their ass and twerking. To be honest, I wasn't the best dancer, but I had sex appeal. Atlanta clients always made it rain and that's exactly what I liked. I was ready to prepare myself to get used to a different crowd and atmosphere. Yet the strip clubs weren't the only thing I had to adjust to.

The first two weeks at my new job was tough. Unlike back home, this pharmacy was 24hrs and had high customer traffic. Constantly being busy took a toll on me, but I was determined to do a good job. My new boss Mrs. Kay was so impressed with my pharmacy skills and work ethic that she gave me a four-dollar raise, after being on the job for just a month With the raise, things started to go in the right direction, I didn't have to worry much about bills. Yet, to maintain the lifestyle I enjoyed I knew it was time to find the right club.

After about two months, I was ready to find a club to work at. I connected with Dee, a long-time friend of my brothers who lived in Atlanta and was familiar with the city. Dee lived in the A for about five years and I knew I could trust him. I asked him to show me around and we set up a couple dates to do so. The first club Dee and I went to was "Pink Pony". It was a mixed club with all different types of ethnicities. The atmosphere felt familiar so I knew it would have worked for me. Unfortunately, it had its downside. The house mom was rude to me from the first day. She didn't like anything about me; my name, the way I danced, or the tattoo on my side, so dancing there did not happen. Dee suggested another club that he and his friends frequented, so we headed there. As we walked through the door all you could see were lights shining and money blowing throughout the room. Clientele were throwing money everywhere and every girl was flooded in cash. It was like a movie. The money had my attention, but the main thing that caught my attention was the rule—clientele could look but they could not touch. I walked over to the bar and asked to speak with the owner.

"Hi, I'm Peaches how may I help you?" said the bartender as she finished cleaning out a glass.

"Hi Peaches. I'm Autumn. Is the owner around? I'm interested in dancing," I said.

"What shift are you looking to work and are you experienced?" she asked.

" Um, I've only danced for about four months, but I catch on fast," I said hoping that this answer would be good enough.

"Look baby, we don't have time for inexperienced girls for night shift..." My once eager smile slowly started to fade. "But day shift you may fit in," she said as she looked me over.

"Okay, okay that will due," I said happy for this option. This is what you need to do Autumn, that's your stage name correct?"

"Yes."

"Ok. This is what you have to do. Head down to the DeKalb County Sheriff's office and apply for an adult entertainment license. It's going to cost $250. The price is different for every county. Once you do that, come back you can start. You got it?"

"Yes, Peaches. I got it."

***

It had been about two months since I received my entertainment dancer licenses and today was my first day working at Club Strokers. At Strokers, the girls weren't friendly. They moved quick and hustled hard, much faster than the pace back home. I needed to stay on top of my game and decided the best way to do that was to stay to myself. In this club the money was hit or miss and it only took one customer to make it a winning night. I got that customer when I met Mr. T.

Mr. T was from New York and owned several businesses in the Atlanta area. The best part about him was he was very generous. He was so giving he even opened a bank account for me and deposited $500 every Friday. The entertainment business became more to me than I could ever imagine. There was so much money involved that it had my full attention to the point I didn't realize it had me wrapped around its finger. I didn't know that it would soon develop into a problem.

My birthday finally arrived, and I was finally turning 21. Lamar finally moved in, and my brother and my family was coming to town. I was extremely excited. August 20' 2004 was going to be the best birthday ever especially because I was having a party. While sitting on the porch, I finished making arrangements for tonight's festivities. I dialed the nightclub to make reservations.

"Hello, Visions Night Club how may I help you?" the receptionist answered.

"Yes, Hi. I would like to make VIP reservations for tonight. It's my twenty-first birthday and I would like two bottles of Moet Champaign and a bottle of Don Perignon."

"Okay sounds great. Can I have a name for the reservation?"

"Yes, Alecia Collins."

"Sounds great we'll see you tonight."

Outside was hot as ever so I went back into the house. Lamar was sitting in the living room watching TV. Although he had been back home for about a month, I had got caught up in my own agenda with working and the club that we hardly spent time with one another.

"Hey Alecia, your brother just called. They are about ten minutes away from the house."

"Yes, I'm so excited!" I squealed. "Did you get a chance to see my dress for tonight?"

"No, but I'll check it out," he said still watching TV.

My dress for tonight was beautiful. Mr.T had bought it for me when he was in New York. He had a trip planned for me this coming weekend as a birthday gift. I couldn't deny the offer so I made arrangements to get away. I just told Lamar I was taking a girls trip with my co-worker Paris. He rarely asked questions anyway. I went into the kitchen to grab a drink when I heard a knock on the door.

"Who is it?" I yelled.

"Open the door, little girl," I heard my brother say on the other side of the door. I went to the door and gave my brother and his girlfriend, Jane a big hug at the sight of him.

"Let me show you two around the house. How was the drive?" I asked

"It was cool," Steve replied. "But I need to get a nap before we go out tonight."

"Okay sounds cool," I said as Lamar and I walked them into the guest room. "This is where you all will be sleeping. Let me know if you all need anything. I gotta go make a run, I'll be back shortly.

I helped them settle in then drove over to my co-worker's Paris house to go over the details of our trip to New York that Mr. T sponsored for us. I needed to go over the flight details, as well as perfect the lie I would tell Lamar. Paris was sitting outside when I pulled up.

"Hey Paris, come to the car. I'm running behind schedule, but need to fill you in on our upcoming trip next week."

"Hey Autumn, Happy birthday beautiful," Paris said leaning over and hugging me. "What's the plan, baby?"

"Okay, we fly out next Friday. My friend, Dee will take us to the airport. I told Lamar we were going to Charlotte, North Carolina for your family reunion, so I'm good."

"Sounds like a plan. Let me know if anything changes, my bag is packed and ready to roll."

"Bet. Sounds good. I'm heading home to get ready for my party tonight at Club Visions. You coming, right?"

"Awe, I want to, but unfortunately I have to work. Have fun though." We exchanged a couple more words then I hugged her goodbye.

I hurried back home to get ready for tonight. Club Visions line was always long even if you had a VIP section. This was one place it was better to be early than late.

"I'm home everybody, who's ready to drink and dance it's my twenty-first birthday," I said as I walked into the house.

"Where have you been?" Lamar asked. "I have been calling your phone for the past hour."

"Oh, I had to run over to Paris's house. She wanted to give me the hotel details for where we'll be staying for her family reunion next weekend," I lied.

"Oh, okay. Well hurry up and get dressed. Everyone's waiting on you." I couldn't tell whether or not he believed me, but I didn't care. Tonight it was all about me.

I showered, touched up my hair then got dressed. When

I put on the dress couldn't help but be mesmerized. Mr. T outdid himself. It was a short black cocktail dress with rhinestones and beads going down the lower back. To complete my outfit, I slid on my satin lace high heels from Nine West and applied my favorite red lipstick. I took one last look in the mirror and was pleased by the reflection. I looked good, and I knew it. I then grabbed my purse and headed out of the bedroom.

"Everyone is waiting on me I assume," I said as I entered the living room. Lamar's eyes lit up which confirmed what I already knew—I looked good.

"You look good sis. Now, let's go," Steve said as everyone began to head out the door."

We all got into the car and headed Visions Night Club which was only fifteen minutes away. Since I ordered about four bottles for the VIP section, we didn't pregame. I didn't want to waste any liquor. But we made sure to party on our way to the club. When we arrived at the club, the line wasn't as bad as I thought. Even better. I was still hype from the car ride and couldn't wait to get inside.

"It's a party, it's a party," I sang as we walk towards the entrance.

"Have ID's ready to check," security shouted.

We handed over our ID's, and for the first time, I didn't have to use someone else's. When we got inside, I went over to the bar to check in our VIP section. The music was jumpin', and I was ready to drink and mingle. There were so many handsome men in the club, and I knew I would grab one. Even though Lamar was with me, I wasn't worried about him. It was my birthday, and it was about me.

The night was moving smooth, and everyone was having a great time. We danced, drank and partied all night. We had been out for almost three hours, and I was drunk and ready to head home. Steve had to head back to Illinois in the morning, so we all decided to leave.

The next morning, I woke up early to cook breakfast. The smell of food must have woken everyone up because they all came into the kitchen. No one could understand how I was up and awake, but everyone was hungry.

"Who wants bacon and eggs with a glass of orange juice?" I asked cheerfully.

"We all do," Lamar yelled out, and everyone laughed.

"Okay sounds good."

When I was finished, we all sat at the table to eat. I was grateful to have my brother Steve with me to help me celebrate my birthday. However, I was even more happy everyone was leaving because I had so much packing to do for my trip to New York. This weekend had been a blast, but the fun wasn't over yet.

***

The week had flown pass and the day arrived for my trip to the Big Apple. Lamar had left for school, and I was packed ready to go. I laid on the couch while I waited on Dee and Paris to head to the airport.

Knock, knock.

"Who is it?" I yelled.

"It's Paris, open up."

"Hey boo what's up are you ready?" I said as opened the door and let her in.

"Hell yea!" she laughed.

"Oh looks who's behind you," I said as I saw Dee car pull up. "Hey Dee," I hollered. "Here we come."

We put our bags in Dee's trunk and were filled with excitement as we sat in his car. Neither one of us had ever been to New York City, so this was going to be an amazing trip. As we pulled up to Hartsfield-Jackson Airport, I couldn't thank Dee enough for the ride.

"Dee, thank you so much. Here are a few dollars for gas," I said as I handed him money.

"You know I got your back Sis," Dee replied.

Our flight landed in Newark Liberty International Airport, Mr.T would pick us up. Paris made a few calls to different dance clubs in New York. No matter what we were all about making some money, even in a different city. While we waited for Mr.T, texted Lamar so he would know we made it to 'North Carolina'. I made sure that my story was airtight. since that was the story.

"Alecia, Lamar going to kick your ass if he finds out you in New York," Paris said teasing me as I lied to Lamar.

"Paris, mind your own business, I got this under control." We went back and forth and also talked about all the things we would do in NY. After waiting two hours Mr. T finally pulled up. outside for him.

"Hey baby," he said as he grabbed our bags.

"Hey," I responded I was a bit annoyed by how late he was but decided to not make a big deal about it. His lateness was the least of my worries.

"How was the flight?" He asked.

"Great. Paris and I are going to pass on what you have planned tonight and check out the city, if that's okay with you."

"Sure Autumn, I'll drop you girls off at the room and talk with you later," he said as he put the last of the bags in the car.

"Okay sounds good." We all got into his car and headed to the hotel.

When we arrived, Paris and I went into the hotel to check in and get dressed. We stayed at the Radisson across the way from the airport. It was a beautiful five-star hotel with a beautiful view. After about four hours, we were finished showered and dressed. I had the receptionist call us a cab to head out on the town.

"Hunts Pointe in the Bronx," Paris said as we entered the cab. I had no idea what she was talking about, but the cab driver did. After about twenty minutes, we pulled up to the address Paris gave cab driver. When I looked outside, I thought it must have been a mistake. My mouth dropped. The area looked scary and unsafe.

"Hunts Point, the Hoe Stroll, "the cab driver attempted to say under his breath but came out more loudly then he intended.

"Oh my God," I said out loud. What did he mean by the 'hoe stroll'? It was obvious we were in the wrong part of town. What made it worse was that the cab driver was rude. He just rushed us out his car.

"Fifty dollars, girls. You two owe me fifty dollars."

I paid him as we got out and grabbed our bags. Once outside all you could smell was cigarette smoke. As we walked towards the strip club and I was utterly disgusted. The clientele looked dirty and ran down. There was no way I was going into this place.

"Paris! There's no way in hell we're going inside there," I said. "Let's call a cab and head to another club to our standards. This place looks horrible."

We got into another taxi and inquired about another Gentleman's Club. The cab driver could tell what type of style we were looking for and took us to another spot.

"The Players Club", he said. "That's maybe more to you girls liking." The Players Club was just five minutes away.

When we arrived, we were very pleased. It was more what we were use too.

"Okay girls, this trip will be ten dollars," the taxi said.

"No problem," Paris responded, "thank you."

We walked inside, and it was perfect. There were beautiful bright lights with chandlers hanging from the ceiling. Unlike the last club, the customers were clean and looked like they had money to blow.

"Hi, how can I help you, girls?" The doorman asked.

"We were wondering if you had any openings for two of us to dance tonight," I asked.

"Sure do. It's amateur night. Come in head to the back and get dressed. All rules and restrictions are on the wall in the dressing room."

Paris and I got dressed. We only had a few hours to hustle the room since we wasted so much time earlier. By the time we were dressed I was over it and ready to go back to the room and relax. Mr. T wouldn't stop texting my phone asking when we were coming back. I wasn't in the mood for him but I knew I had to play nice.

"You ready Autumn?" Paris asked.

"You know it. Let's get paid."

Back home, we doubled team customers to get all their money. I did all the talking while she did the rubbing. It worked every time. Tonight would be no different. We walked out to the dance floor and saw our first victim and went over to approach him.

"Hey baby. How are you?" I said as I sat on his lap and Paris rubbed on his chest.

"Great. What's your name? he asked.

"Autumn, and this is my girlfriend Paris. How about a dance or two?"

"Sounds good to me," he replied.

I didn't care to ask him for his name. I called all the customers baby. We headed back into the VIP dance room. As we walked back, with one of us on each side of him, we were able to talk him into booking two hours, which was six-hundred dollars apiece. This club was definitely worth it.

At the end of the night, we headed back to the hotel. the club had its own cab service which was great, because those last taxi rides were expensive. When we arrived at the hotel Mr.T was waiting on me . He also booked an extra room for Paris.

"How was your night?" He asked as I entered the room.

"It was okay. We didn't make any money, but you'll take care of me right?" I flirted as I rubbed his head. I lied about us not making money because I knew he would give me about two-thousand dollars—enough for me to even give Paris since she came along and missed work.

"Don't worry about it Autumn, I'll take care of you," he promised.

"I also have dinner planned for us all tomorrow evening since you'll be leaving early Sunday morning."

"Sounds good," I responded.

I showered and got into bed. I felt Mr. T climb in bed with me. I did not want to lay in the bed. This was not in my plans. All I could do was close my eyes and hope he didn't touch me. "What in the world did I get myself into?" I said to myself as I tightly clenched my legs closed together. Although I didn't want to, this was business. Mr.T was infatuated with me so whatever was about to go down I was going to make sure I got it over and done with quick so he would give me my money.

The next morning, I was awaken by the sound of snores. I turned over to my right and saw Mr.T laying on the side of me. "Yuck," I said to myself. I quickly got up to check on Paris who was in the room next door.

Knock, Knock.

"Open the door Paris! Open up. Get up, and let me in," I said while continuously knocking.

"What's up girl, everything okay?" she asked.

"Girl no, I'm ready to go."

"I figured that," she replied laughing.

"Here, thanks for coming," I said as I handed her a wad of money.

Mr.T had given me five-hundred dollars to compensate Paris time for coming along with me—like I said, he was generous.

"Oh thanks, Autumn," Paris said as she took the money. "Tell that old man thank you too," she laughed.

"Girl, shut up, and get dress I don't feel like being bothered with him this morning," I said as I hugged her. She laughed. Although Mr. T was my sugar daddy, I could not deal with the thought of him touching me.

I went back into my room and Mr.T had ordered room service for us both. The aroma from the sausage patties smelled so good and I was starving.

"Sit down and eat Autumn, I have to get going. I have some business to attend to, but I'll see you girls later this evening as planned."

"Okay see you tonight baby," I responded as I grabbed my plate.

Paris and I stayed and chilled in the hotel for the

remainder of the day. I had about $2,300 total from the Strip Club and Mr. T. I was happy but all I could think about was going home. It was a short trip, and worth it. We didn't have to pay for a single thing. That was the luxury of having a Sugar Daddy, and he made it all worth it.

7
IT'S A GIRL

Atlanta officially became home for me. I was getting around the city just fine and met more people than I could ever imagine—good folks with southern hospitality and high ambition. The weather was always nice and the sun always shined. This was more of the reason why I had so much energy to want to work hard and build my own empire.

Lamar and I loved going out to eat on Sunday evenings. Mostly because it was the only day that worked with my schedule since I worked seven days a week. We often went to my favorite restaurant, Houston's Steakhouse. Their salmon and baked potato was something to die for. The restaurant was upscale and a lot of celebrities would dine there. A typical bill for a party of two would be around a couple hundred dollars. With the lifestyle, I like to live; I always kept plenty of money that way I could splurge.

One evening after dinner I felt a little under the weather. I just couldn't hold anything down. I was on birth control so the idea of being pregnant never crossed me. Lamar insisted we go to the emergency room to get me checked out. As we headed to the hospital my mind was racing. "What if I am pregnant?" I silently asked myself. I thought of all the things I wouldn't be able to do, especially dancing. A pregnancy could ruin my future. After getting checked in we waited on the doctor. The doctor came into the room with a smile from cheek to cheek.

"Congratulations. You two are having a baby!" he said excitedly. I took a deep breath and busted out in tears. Lamar was overly excited and couldn't understand why I was crying. Don't get me wrong I was happy, I just was not ready. This was bad timing. There was so much more I needed to accomplish. I knew Lamar would make a great father especially since this would be his first child, it just happened to fast.

Everything eventually started to change. My stomach began to grow, my face started to get chunky, and I could no longer hide the pregnancy. I eventually had to stop dancing. Mr. T noticed my absence and started reaching out. He would call my phone but I just wouldn't answer. His calls wouldn't stop so after a month had gone by I decided to pick up.

"Hello, how are you Mr. T?"

"Autumn are you okay, what in the world is wrong with your phone? I've called you several times within the last month and even stopped by the club. Is everything okay?"

"Um, not quite. Maybe we should do lunch or dinner, if that's okay with you," I suggested.

"Yes, yes darling. As soon as possible, I've just been worried about you and also had a gift for you as well. How about tomorrow over in Buckhead at Houston's Restaurant?"

"Yes Mr.T, that will do. 6 pm will work for me."

"Sounds great see you then."

The next day after work I went straight to the restaurant. When I walked into the restaurant, I saw him already seated at a table.

"Good evening Mr. T. How are you?" I said as I approached him.

"Autumn, Autumn," he said as he lifted his head up and smiled. "You are glowing beautiful and I'm sure I know why," he said as he looked down at my baby bump.

Mr. T knew right away without me saying a word what I had been hiding. "Alecia" he said, "I know you're pregnant."

My face dropped. I was embarrassed only because he believed so much in me and how I carried myself as a businesswoman in this industry of dancing. The many times we had dinner I would share my ideas with him of opening my own boutique. He wasn't just my loyal customer he was a friend.

"Yes I am Mr. T. As you can see there's no way I can hide this baby bump, but it's going to be okay."

"Autumn I do understand, but you have so much drive and hustle in you. Are you sure this is what you're ready for?"

I thought about what he was asking me for about a minute before I replied.

"Yes, actually this is what I may need to slow me down. I will get to focus on doing something more respectful with my life."

"Understandable my dear," Mr. T responded.

After dinner, he handed me an envelope before walking out the restaurant.

"Autumn I have something for you, and I also want you to know how much I love you and wish the best for you and your new edition."

"Thank you Mr. T, I love you as well and thank you for everything," I said as I took the envelope from him and hugged him. He kissed me on my forehead and we said our goodbyes. That was the last time we spoke and seen one another.

***

Driving back home towards Marietta, my fingers kept twitching from the anticipation of what was inside the envelope. *How much money is in here?* I thought to myself. The anticipation was killing me so I pulled over. I carefully and slowly opened the envelope not wanting to damage what was inside. As I pulled the check out the envelope I could see two digits and a coma.

"Holy shit!" I yelled out loud.

The check was in the amount of $10,000. I didn't understand what it was for, but I was ecstatic and at a loss for words.

"Wow, wow, thank you Mr. T. Thank you," I repeated as I got back on the road.

***

My pregnancy was rolling along, and Lamar and I were doing great. We were so happy about having a baby girl. The pregnancy made us closer to one another and sparked conversations about getting married. Lamar wasn't your average guy—he wasn't too fond of the idea of a "baby mama". He wanted a family. I knew it was only right to give the man what he had always wanted. Excited about our new life, we set a date to get married—June 18th, Lamar's birth day. He wanted to get married before we had the baby so our family was official.

Living in Atlanta and planning a wedding back in Peoria

was work, but with the money I saved and the money Mr.T had given me I knew I would have the prettiest and biggest wedding any girl who was expecting a baby could have. Lamar and I had a wedding party of 28 people in total. It was a day of love and laughter and one of the best days of my life. It was also the day I committed myself to him and only him. Although I had infidelity issues, I prayed God would steer me into the right direction.

***

I was now a married woman, pregnant and ready to deliver. When my due date arrived—August 11th – I couldn't have been more ready; however, my baby girl had other plans. My doctor advised to wait another week and if no progress was made I would have to be induced. That was the longest week of my life. Every day Lamar and I walked and exercised hoping it would help induce labor but it didn't. With no luck, I was called in to be induced. On August 20th and at 9pounds 12 ounces, Jalyssa Christine was born. What was even more amazing was that she was born on my 22nd birthday! My first born and I shared the same birthday, how amazing was that! That day, my life changed forever. Being a new mother I looked forward to teaching my daughter the right way of life and raising her to be a sweet young lady. Motherhood showed me that it was time for me to change my life for the better and become more of a lady that respected herself. I was ready to do whatever it took to live the right way, even quitting the entertainment business for good.

A year into marriage was more than I imagined. The duties of being both a new mother and wife were wearing me out. I couldn't quite adjust to the change as smoothly as I imagined. What made it even more difficult was that I worked almost seven days a week. It became too much and I was ready to throw the towel in. We didn't have any family in Georgia that was close to us to help provide support, so all the responsibilities fell on the two of us. If it wasn't for my girlfriend, Ann, I would have completely lost it. She was from my hometown of Peoria and she dated my friend Dee; that's how we met. We became close friends and even shared play dates with the kids. Whenever things were rough with Lamar she was always there to listen.

Lamar and I went through issues of "growing up". He wanted to party every weekend and I couldn't stand it. Having a new baby and a smaller income no longer allowed that type of lifestyle, yet he didn't understand that. We constantly argued about bills and money. I tried to be as patient as possible but my patience wore thin. When we first moved to Atlanta my money stayed a flow and I had plenty in the bank. Yet, we went from living in a two bedroom townhouse to a one bedroom apartment. It just didn't add up. Lamar would soon graduate with a Bachelors in Accounting so I knew it would pay off later if I just held on. Yet, his actions did not help, In fact they made things worst. I was ready to move back to Peoria where I had family support.

I've worked since I was fourteen years old and was always able to care for myself without struggling so financial problems stressed me out. The thought of potentially getting the electricity or water cut off was all I could think about and I refused to let that happen. As a young child, I experienced this. My brother and I never knew what we were going to come home next—whether it was no lights, no food, or no water. The memories were traumatizing and I vowed to never live like that. That is why I hustled and did whatever it took to never experience that again. Having financial difficulties terrified me and it seemed with Lamar, I was living my worst nightmare.

After months of trying to stick it out, I couldn't take it any longer. Enough was enough. I called Steve and let him know what Lamar and I were going through. I asked to move in with him so I could save some money and get back on my feet. Steve would never turn his back on me. He had an apartment where he hardly stayed so I knew it would work out.

I had just made it home from work after picking up my daughter, Jalyssa, from Ann's house. My baby girl was getting so chunky. Her fat legs had the cutest rolls. she loved for me to play Patty Cake with her.

" Patty cake, patty cake", "Roll'em up, put them in a pan," I sang to her as we played when we reached home. We both laughed. As we were playing, Lamar walked into the house. It was time for us to sit down once and for all to have a serious discussion regarding our marriage.

"Hey my loves," Lamar said to us both.
" Hey sweetie, " I replied "Listen we need to talk and it can't wait."

I put Jalyssa into her walker while I waited for Lamar to finish change out of his work clothes.

"Yes, Alecia what's on your mind?"

This was going to be a tough conversation to have, especially since Lamar was such a family man, he loved his family unconditionally. However, when it came to the responsibilities of being the man of the house he fell short.

"Look baby, we've run into a lot of financial issues lately.

It's even caused us to borrow money from Steve. This is not what I moved here to Atlanta for. Damn it Lamar. I need you to be a man, a real man that handles business, like Mr. T - I mean like a real man should," I said hoping he didn't catch what I said.

"Mr.T? Alecia who in the hell is Mr. T?" Lamar said angrily. I started to answer but he stopped me. "You know what Alecia, your ass think you slick. I've sat back long enough and allowed you to come and go and do what you want. I don't care what you do from here, just don't take Jalyssa away from me."

"Well, Lamar, I'm moving back to Peoria. I'm sick and tired living from check to check. I'm used to a certain lifestyle that you just can't give me. There's certain desires I have, you know clothes, shoes, trips, money. Damn it all of that," I shouted.

"Calm the hell down Alecia. Those are material items. What in the hell is wrong with you?" he shouted. "I knew that dancing bullshit stripping lifestyle was going to get the best of you and take over your head. I don't care what you do just leave me the hell alone okay, leave me alone," he yelled before slamming the door walking out. I knew he was hurt but there was no turning back.

The conversation was over. I had my mind already made up. I loved Lamar with all my heart yet, we were broke and struggling. I couldn't deal with it. The strip club was no longer an option. I swore to myself I would never dance again; I couldn't got back to that lifestyle. I also could no longer stay here. This was not the life I imagined, so it was time for me to pack up and head back to Peoria.

For the following weeks, I made sure everything was in position for the move. I transferred my CVS Pharmacy position back to my previous store in Peoria and solidified my move. With that out the way it was time to figure out how to make some quick cash.

8

LET'S GET IT

It wasn't long before I started clubbing again. Every weekend I was out trying to distract myself for the stress built up from my marriage. I just needed a drink—almost every night. Everything I promised myself that I would do when I moved back didn't happen. I didn't even begin to start. It was easier to escape then deal with what was happening in my life. I was depressed. I knew it, and Steve witnessed it. Within two months of being back, Steve was telling me to go back to Lamar.

"Sis, give it a chance. Lamar is really a great guy, and you two have a family. Sometimes something worth having takes time. He's working towards building a foundation for you three, something we never had growing up."

I knew Steve meant well, but Lamar's finances were interfering with our bills, and it was stressing me out. It reminded me too much of how I grew up and how much I went without. I certainly didn't want to relive that life over again. I couldn't handle it. I knew in my heart Steve made sense. What he was saying was true. Maybe I should try to work through it with Lamar.

"Brother, you're absolutely right. I am going to return to Atlanta a make my marriage work. If I have to, I'll pick up extra hours or even get another job. I know Lamar means well and loves his family, so I'll give it a shot. If I still have to return, later on I know you'll be here for me."

Everything I wanted out of this move never happened. Steve was right. I couldn't get focused because I missed Lamar so much. I hate how Lamar and I ended things. To make matters worse, I was broke. My hours at CVS were cut because the store hours weren't the same as Atlanta. No matter how much I tried, the reality was Atlanta had more opportunities. It was time for me to take full advantage of it all.

I reached out to my job back in Atlanta and my Supervisor Mrs. Kay allowed me to have my job back. If that was one thing I made sure to do was to always leave on a good note with employers; you never know when the time will come when you actually need them. After a few days of tying some loose ends, I was finally on my way back to Atlanta.

As I drove back to Atlanta, I reached out to Ann to give her the news.

"Hello," she answered

"Hey Ann! Guess what? I'm on my way back to the Atl," I said through the phone. I was elated, but I didn't want to yell because Jalyssa was sleeping in the back.

"What girl to visit?" Ann asked.

"No to live. I couldn't adjust in Peoria and hardly made any money so I'm back with a plan and I know you won't mind being a part of it," I said anxious to tell her my new scheme.

"Girl, what do you have going on now?"

"You'll see, once I get settled in I'll pick you up and we'll talk things over."

"Okay Alecia," she said as she laughed. " I'll talk to you soon."

Ann was thrilled to have me back and I was looking forward on hooking up with her after I settled in. She had no idea of what I was about to proposition her with. But if Ann knew me she knew it involved making some quick cash. The difference with this plan was that we would be risking our lives. But I wasn't worried, I had it all figured out.

After ten hours of driving, I finally made it back to Atlanta. Lamar moved into a one bedroom apartment in Powder Springs, Georgia, which wasn't it too far from where I worked in Smyrna, Georgia. To be honest, I liked the area a lot more than where we used to live. We were now closer to my preferred grocery store Publix which had a great fruit selection—my family loved fruit. As I pulled up to the front of the apartment complex I could see Lamar waiting outside. I knew he was eager to see Jalyssa; he was happy to have his baby girl back home. As for me, we planned on taking it one day at a time.

"Hey, Lamar we made it back safely," I said as I greeted him, with Jalyssa on my arm.

"Yes, I'm glad to have you back," he said forcing a smile. He then quickly turned his attention to Jalyssa, "Hey daddy's baby. Come to daddy big girl." Jalyssa jumped out of my grip and into Lamar's arm. I know she missed her daddy, I missed him too. It was nice to see them reconnect. For a few moments I just took in the sight of their embrace. I was brought back to reality when a text came through on my phone. It was Ann.

"Umm, Lamar, I need to unpack the car and head over

to Ann's right quick, you mind?" I asked him.

"Do what you want Alecia, I got Jalyssa," he responded while keeping his focus on Jalyssa.

"Okay, thanks."

I hurried up and unpacked the car, then kissed Jalyssa goodbye.

"Mommy will be right back ok baby. Lamar, I'm gone. I'll be back soon."

I headed north towards Acworth, Georgia where Ann lived. My nerves were bad. I didn't know if Ann would agree or not I just knew she could used the money. The closer I got to Ann's, the more sweat drenched my face. I knew she would think I was crazy but I needed her so the plan could run smooth.

Knock, Knock.

"Who is it?" Ann yelled from the other side of the door.

"Alecia. Girl, open the door." I heard the locks unlock and the door swung open. Ann stood there with the biggest grin on her face. It felt good to be back home. She reached her arm and I went into her embrace.

"What's up girl, give me a hug. Come in here and sit down. tell me what in the hell you have up your sleeve now," she said as she guided me to her living room.

"Girl, you remember when I worked at Stroker's about four years ago right?" I asked as we made ourselves comfortable on her couch.

"Yea, what about it."

"Well, I had met this guy named Ben. He invited me over to his house a few times in Smyrna. Anyhow he was loaded in cash! He always had money and jewelry lying around the house."

"Okay Alecia, and where you going with this?"

"You already know. I want us to go over and hang out with him and snatch everything." Ann's eyes grew big.

"Alecia hell no! What if he catches us or it don't go as planned?" she asked surprised by my proposition.

"Look Ann, it will work out. It has to. I'm broke as hell. When I was back in Peoria all I did was go out every night and spend all my money on bullshit. I haven't been in this bad of a shape in a very long time," I confessed, hoping she would be willing to join me. Ann shook her head.

"Alecia, if we do this how much money you think we could get?"

"At least fifty-thousand. That's not including every piece of merchandise he has laying around. We taking that too!" We both started laughing. I knew she was in.

"Okay, I'm in. Let's do it. girl you insane."

"Sounds good. I'll reach out to Ben on my way home and see what's up for this Saturday."

"Saturday? Alecia that's in a couple of days," Ann said.

"I know, so get prepared. I'll go over more details once I speak with Ben," I said as I stood up to leave. "I'm gotta head out so close the door behind me." We both hugged and she walked me out the door. The plan was in action.

While driving home I was relieved that Ann agreed to join me. Four eyes were always better than two, and with the experience I had from the entertainment business, it would be a piece of cake. All I had to do was play him like Paris and I used to play our tricks. Warm him up and lead him to believe we were going to have a good time. If that was one thing I learned being a dancer, the power of the pussy is real. This would be easy. I gave Ben a call and he fell right into the trap. Saturday was locked in. It was time to get paid.

***

Saturday quickly rolled around and before I knew it the plan was in action.. Lamar had made plans to take Jalyssa over to a friend's house with their daughter for a play date, which worked out perfectly for me. He didn't really care about what I did anymore, so offering an explanation was unnecessary. After I got dressed I prepped a bottle full of assorted over the counter pain pills. I needed those for tonight's plan .

At about 9pm I pulled up to Ann's house to pick her up. We were ready. As we merged unto the highway to head towards Ben's, I went over the plan with Ann.

"Look Ann, this is how the night will go. I'll have Ben constantly drinking all night. We're only going to have one drink—sip slow. After Ben is on his about third drink, I'll slip him about four pills in his fourth one. That way we put him out to sleep. And when I say out, he'll be comatose."

"Alecia, are you sure this will work?" Ann asked sounding a bit worried.

"Yes, Ann, damn. Once he starts drinking that fourth drink asks him if you could used his bathroom. It's across from his bedroom. Pay attention to everything you see: money, chains, and watches anything of value. " Ann shook her head letting me know she was ready.

"Okay, let's go!" she said.

We pulled up to Ben's Place ten minutes later. When we parked I made sure I had the pills and touched up our makeup.

"Okay, Ann, are you ready?"

"Yep, let's get him."

We walked up to Ben's apartment . His music was

blasting so much that we could hear it from the parking lot. I was sure he was ready for some action with the both of us. The thought of it made me laugh. He was about to have a rude awakening.

Knock, Knock.

"Who is it?" Ben yelled, while opening the door. When he saw us at the door a smile stretched across his face. *Poor fool.*

"Ladies, ladies, how are you two? Come inside," he said as he licked his lips.

As soon as we stepped inside it was game time. Ann followed me in while following instructions as given. We looked around took note on what was of value within arm's reach. It wasn't long before we pumped up the volume in Ben's apartment. Especially me. I was drinking and singing every song that came on the radio, making sure I gave the persona that we were here for a good time. Ann was doing what she had been told and sat back and waited to make her move.

"It's a party in here," Ben yelled over the loud music.

"Yes it is ," Ann replied. "let's keep drinking," she said as she looked at me. It was time.

I reached in my back pocket for the pills while him and Ann danced throughout the living room. He was so hypnotized by her presence that he paid no attention to what I was doing.

"Let's drink," I yelled out, handing Ben his fourth drink spiked with my pills.

Ben took that drink to the head in one gulp. *Perfect.* Ann was still in Ben's face and pulled him closed then asked to used the bathroom.

"Hey handsome, where's the bathroom?"

"Upstairs baby," Ben replied in a drunken state while falling back on to the couch.

"Everything okay Ben?" I asked faking a sense of concern.

"Yes Autumn, everything is o--," he slurred. Before he could finish his sentence, he was out.

"Ben, Ben," I said as I shook him on the shoulder. There was no waking him up. He was out.

"Ann, get down here," I yelled. I heard her footsteps come into the living room.

"What's up, is he sleep?"

"Yes, let's move fast and quietly."

I moved as fast as I could upstairs to his bedroom while Ann was downstairs grabbing what she could. The clock was ticking and my adrenaline was high. I flipped over his mattress, pulled out dresser drawers, looked inside his furnace registers, no place was left untouched. Anywhere I could think he would hide money, I checked. When I got to the last drawer in his dresser I moved all the clothes aside and saw a black plastic bag. I grabbed it and opened it and knew I hit the jackpot. Inside was nothing but stacks of money rolled up. It had to be thousands. The bag was so heavy that I needed Ann's help to carry out.

"Ann, get up here now," I loudly whispered.

"What's up girl?" She said as she walked in. Her hands were full and I knew we robbed him clean. "Let's go now I got everything that looked of value. Let's go before this dude wakes up and kills the both of us."

"Okay, okay help me with this bag," I said as I showed her the money. We grabbed our things and rushed out the apartment and down the stairs into my car. I could feel my heart beat pounding through my chest. Ann looked like she was on a high. We robbed his ass!

"Oh my God," Ann yelled as she shut the car door behind her. Without putting our seatbelts on, I peeled off.

"Oh my God is right," I replied.

"He's going to wake up Alecia and notice all his money and jewelry is gone and come find us," she said with worry I her voice.

"Ann stop worrying. Atlanta is big as hell. He won't know where to begin to look for us at," I assured her. This was a fool proof plan and I made sure of it.

We quickly drove back to Ann's home. I couldn't help but wonder how much money we had in the bag. From what I could tell, I was sure it was more than twenty-thousand in cash and maybe over fifty-thousand in jewelry. Whatever it was, we were going to split it even. .

"Alecia, you hadn't told anyone about this have you," Ann asked as we pulled up to her house.

"Ann, no girl. You worry too much. Relax it's okay," I said trying to calm her nerves.

We grabbed everything and went inside Ann's house to count the money. I was eager to see how much we made but Ann was nervous. She kept looking over her shoulder. I just laughed. It was normal to feel how she was. She just committed a robbery.

"We can go in my living room to count the money. No one's home," she said as we walked through the door.

We dumped out the bag with the money and jewelry that Ann had grabbed. After everything was spread out, we unraveled all the money and began to count. It seems like we counted forever until we finally finished. At the end we had almost $40,000 dollars in cash! That didn't even include the jewelry. To be honest, I didn't want any parts of the jewelry so I let Ann keep that. Jewelry and merchandise could be traced back. That is not what we needed, especially not me.

"Looks like we get $20,000 a piece Ann. You can have the jewelry, I'll pass on that."

"$20,000! Alecia, girl I'm getting my car fix and taking the kids to Six Flags," Ann yelled. She couldn't believe it. We were surrounded by money. Her living room floor turned green.

"Ann, this stays between me and you. Seriously, don't start splurging and spending a bunch of money. Hold on to some of it and save it in case of an emergency."

"Okay, Alecia you're right. Damn girl you crazy, but thank you. I definitely need this money." We began to pack the money back in bands and split it even. Ann put all the jewelry in a bag and we stood up from the floor letting out big stretches.

"I'm going to go ahead and go to bed we've had a long night I'll talk with you soon," she said as she cracked her back. It had been a long night. We were both tired.

"Sounds good. Love you girl. I'm headed home." I hugged her grabbed my half of the money and headed out the door.

As I got into the car to head home the idea of what just took place didn't even dawn on me. Money was always the motive. I would always do whatever it took to take care of mine and this situation was a clear example of that. I didn't care if I had to put my life on the line. And I sure did not give a damn what anyone thought about it—even Lamar.

9
THE BUST

Life with Lamar never got any better. In fact, it felt like a waste of time. I thought moving back would help rekindle our relationship and fix things but it didn't. Not to my expectations. It took him longer than planned to finish school which left all the financial responsibility of managing the house on me. I was doing 75% of the work which was exhausting and I no longer had any patience. I couldn't take it anymore. Our marriage was over. It wasn't all Lamar's fault, I admit, I was partly to blame. When we first started dating I spoiled Lamar. I handled all the bills and my own personal needs and gave him a pass to not step up to the plate. This crippled him and in turn crippled our relationship. Since then our relationship began to crumble. As much as we tried to save it, it was no used. I thought building a family would help but it didn't. Nothing could change the way I felt. It was finally over so I began to make plans to move on—without him.

On April 1st 2007, I moved back to Peoria. I filed for divorce and left my life in Atlanta behind. This time moving back home came with peace. I was happy about going back home to my mom and my brother Steve. Coming home provided the opportunity to talk business. He shared that he started investing and buying property and I wanted in. Everyone around him was getting money and living good. There was major boss moves in motion and I wanted to be a part of it.

When I moved back home I lived at Steve's apartment. With all my belongings, the apartment became tight. I knew I would need to find my own place soon. I lived there, but Steve ran his business out of the apartment. He always had his guys over to talk business which always involved some money exchange. Steve would have me re-count money to double check his count. It would take forever; and seeing that amount of money would have my nerves bad. I would try to count as quickly and as accurate as possible and be as accurate as possible. Once I counted $250,000 by hand. It was a ridiculous amount but I understood the game.

Hustling was designed to survive and build. Once you made a substantial amount of money you could eventually step away and invest your savings into assets. This was the best move but not always the easiest. You never knew who was watching you or out to get you and this street game was far from fair, everyone was suspect.

I connected with my home girl Kia who filled me in on everything that was going on around the town. She mentioned she was going back to college which I thought was great. There was nothing wrong with wanting more and I was happy to finally see her chasing her dream. We were grown women and it was time for change. I had dreams of my own. I wanted to open my own Boutique which would carry handbags, accessories, and shoes. Steve had the money to invest which helped put my plan in motion. I had it all mapped out. I was well connected with the wholesale distributors out of Atlanta so inventory wasn't a problem and the rental units in Peoria were reasonable; we wouldn't pay much for a storefront. My boutique was my focus and I put my time and energy into making that dream a reality. As time went on, things were looking up and I was very excited. I couldn't imagine anything going wrong.

One day after work, as I headed to my mom's house to pick up Jalyssa, I noticed that I had four missed calls from an unavailable caller.

"Umm, that's strange," I said out loud while driving. *Ring. Ring.*

"Hello," I answered.

"You have a collect call from Steve, would you except?" said the operator.

"Yes I will." I was sure the sound of my heartbeat could be heard through the phone. The blood from my face flushed out as I tried to remain my composure. With two click sounds I heard Steve on the other line.

"What in the hell are you doing in jail Steve?" I shouted into the receiver. I couldn't contain it. Worry and anger consumed me.

"Look sis, some bull happened. I need you to do exactly what I say. Go get a cashier's check in the amount of $20,000," Steve requested.

"What! $20,000?" I repeated shocked.

"Yes, $20k. Get that money and bail me out." He let me know where I could get the money and before we could say our goodbyes the phone cut off. "$20K bail," I said to myself out loud. *Steve what the hell did you do?*

***

"Hi, I'm here to bail out Collins," I said to the officer.

"His bond is $20,000 would you like to leave money on his books?" the officer asked with a sarcastic attitude. Ignoring his attitude, I reached into my purse.

"No, I'll like to bond him out now," I said as I laid down the cashier's check on the counter.

"Oh, ok," the officer nervously replied as he looked at the cashier's check, "I will get his paperwork ready and he'll be out shortly." It was apparent he was in disbelief.

I sat patiently waiting for Steve to be released, I couldn't help but bite my nails. The environment had my nerves out of whack.

About an hour after posting bail Steve came walking out behind the metal doors. I ran up to him and gave him a hug, relieved to know he was ok.

"What in the hell is going on, Steve?" I whispered.

"Thanks, sis, for coming. I'll tell you about it when we get into the car," he said as he gently tugged on my arm leading me out of the prison.

We both rushed into the car leaving the premises. Steve was quiet and for the first time ever, he looked worried. I knew whatever happened was serious. I couldn't take the silence any longer. I needed to know what was going on.

"What in the hell is going on Steve? Talk to me. NOW," I pleaded.

"Look Alecia, I got pulled over and had an ounce of marijuana on me. I thought I would be ok, but it wasn't the state troopers. They were federal agents."

"THE FEDS?" I shouted. *How could this be happening?*

"Yes Alecia. It's been a lot of snitching going on back in Peoria and I believe my name is in cahoots' with a lot of it, especially with people I had dealings with. They had caught drug cases and now they're telling on me."

I couldn't believe my ears. This could not be happening. Steve was my protector. Now he was going to jail? And it's all because someone snitched. Tears began to cloud my view.

"Sis, I just want you to be prepared for the worst. I might get indicted," he continued.

"What is 'indicted' Steve?" He was silent. "No Lord, this can't happen. Steve you are all we got to hold this family together. Who's going to step in and do your job?" I said as the tears rushed out. Steve reached over and grabbed my hand.

"Alecia, calm down. An indictment means a formal charge or accusation of a crime. If I do go down and the feds pick me up you are intelligent enough to make sure everything and everyone is taking care of."

"Steve, the indictment…does that have something to do with why your bond was twenty-thousand dollars?" I asked as I wiped the tears from my eyes.

"I don't know, Alecia. I just have a bad feeling that I might be going to jail for a long time."

***

Boom. Boom. Boom.

I awoke to a loud noise and bright lights which flashed in my face as I slept on the couch.

"GET DOWN ON YOUR KNEES NOW. NOW I SAID," I heard a voice say. It came from behind the gun which pointed directly at me. I was hardly awake. My eyes were still stuck together from the crust from in between them.

"WHERE IS HE?" the police shouted.

I didn't say anything. I was in complete shock. I couldn't understand what was happening. One minute I was sleeping, the next I had a revolver pointed at my head while another officer handcuffed me. Within minutes, over thirty police officers surrounded me. The apartment was being raided just days after I bailed Steve out of jail. They questioned me, but no words could come out. My body was stiff as they walked me out the apartment. They dragged me down the stairs, and I felt numb. All I could feel was the ice-cold handcuffs around my wrist. Where was Steve?

I was taken into the police station for questioning. As I walked in, my heart sank as I saw federal agents walking in with Steve from another entrance. He looked my way and bent his head down in shame. This was happening.

"Mrs. Collins, we have a few questions. This will go well as long as you are honest, do you understand?" the officer said as he took the handcuffs off in the interview room

I knew whatever they asked not to answer without having a lawyer present. I kept silent as I rubbed my wrist relieving the pressure of the handcuffs.

"Alecia, we know your involvement, and we need you to show us where the stash house is located."

"Stash house?" I questioned. There was no way I would give that up. "Officer, I don't know what you're talking about, and I want my phone call to contact my attorney."

"With further a due, if you're not willing to cooperate we have no other choice to book you and take you to the Peoria County Jail."

"For what?" I yelled. "This can't be legal! You don't have me doing anything!" I shouted. I was furious.

"Book her, Officer D.," the investigator instructed.

Within minutes I was back in handcuffs and escorted out of the room.

My arrest didn't last long. My cousin Frank came to bail me out, and I had him take me back to the apartment. The ten o'clock news came on, and the first report was about an eight-man indictment the city had served that day. An indictment which involved my brother and seven other guys. They were all charged with conspiracy and money laundering over a five-year investigation. The news plastered their faces all over the television screen. When I saw Steve's face, the humiliation cut me deep. So much so it made me vomit over and over. Steve was facing twenty years to life. He was only twenty-eight years old at the time. His life quickly shifted went from fame to shame. It was the beginning of a nightmare for us all.

**

Steve awaited trial for over a year. The back and forth from Chicago to see his lawyer and the visits to the county were wearing me out. I was so depressed. What made it even more stressful, I was pregnant. I began dating this guy Jermaine and we were having a baby. On top of everything going on, the last thing I needed was to be having another child.

Finally, the day came for my brother to get sentenced. My family stood outside the courtroom where my aunt prayed relentlessly over for fairness and righteousness. Steve was facing up to twenty years. We hoped the judge would show him favor since he never had a record. As the court settled, the room went silent and the judge had Steve stand up as he read his charges.

"In the case of Collins verse the United States, I order you to serve 238-months in the United States Federal Bureau."

"NO! NO! NO!" I cried out. I went into a total outcry. I was immediately removed from the court room for my outrage and taken outside. It felt like my heart had been cut out and I had bled to death. Never had I been at my weakest. My brother was just sentenced to two decades behind bars. This was the moment I had to pull myself together and do it fast. I had to become everything he had taught me and take care of our family--my mother, my children, and his children. My brother was depending on me as I always depended on him. It was clear I had no choice. I had to change lanes.

10
THE TRANSITION

Who would have ever imagined that the time would fly past so quickly, I finally made it to see my thirties? Steve was still incarcerated; something we never fully got used to.

Steve receiving a twenty-year sentence changed my life forever. Even after four years our family never got used to it. After two years of being incarcerated, Steve transferred to Yazoo City, Mississippi. One thing I learned about the Federal System was that they would place you anywhere in the United States, no matter rather if you have family there or not. The system was designed to keep you far away from your love ones as possible. However, I didn't let this get in my way. I made sure we visited Steve often no matter how far the drive was.

In that time, I gave birth to my baby boy Orlando making me a mother of two children and responsible for a total of seven kids. I made sure to look out for my brothers five children while he was serving time. Life was crazy.

I continued to work at the Pharmacy but as time went on it no longer provided what I needed. Working with the company was moving nowhere. The drive to stay was dead and the money was slow. With my new responsibilities of caring for the family, I decided to go back on my word from four years prior. I went back to dancing. I worked at Kap's Gentleman Club for a few years before I finally quit dancing once and for all. I saved $30,000 and was ready to move forward with future plans.

With the new changes, I struggled with the decision of enrolling back into college or focusing once again on opening up my own business. It was important that I made the right choice. So much time had passed an I wanted to think like a responsible adult and mother.

A month passed since I quit the gentlemen's club and I had no clue what to do next; but, I had money saved up to invest. There was a co-worker by the name of Taylor who worked at Kap Gentleman's Club with me. Year's prior, she had opened her own commercial cleaning business so I decided to reach out to her and ask a few questions.

"Hello, may I speak with Taylor?"

"Yes this is she speaking, who am I speaking with?"

"Taylor it's Autumn. How are you?"

"Girl couldn't be better. Blessed actually since I no longer work at the club."

"That's why I'm calling, I'm interested in starting my own cleaning service and could used some tips on how to get it started," I said.

"Oh girl no problem, do you have a paper and pen?"

Taylor sat me down and schooled me on everything I needed to know to start. She was insightful and patient and answered any question I had. Things started to come together. Once we hung up, I had laser focus. I mapped out a business plan that entailed everything I would need: how I would attract customers, services I would offer, prices I would charge and more. The plan took me exactly one week to develop before it was finalized.

For the first time, I took my time to build something from only an idea and follow through with it. I was proud of myself. All these years I worried about money and maintaining an image. Now, much older and experienced I no longer cared about those things. I became a believer to the belief and reality of what happens when you have faith and trust in God no matter what.

After a year of getting my cleaning service off the ground, service was moving in the right direction and I was overjoyed. With my business, I knew I would be able to help my family and brother once he came home especially since he would be a convicted felon. What was even more of a blessing; I invested money into rental properties so he wouldn't have to worry about a place to stay either. By the grace of God everything was falling into place, the values my brother taught me as a young girl started to serve me now as a woman.

***

As the years went by, more blessings came through. President Obama was in office and he was ready to make change with the federal prison system. The system was unfair. Many individuals were railroaded with obscene sentences for first-time convictions; this was the case of my brother's. The system would sentence you for less time for cocaine than for crack. This reality immediately isolated a lot of individuals. It unfairly put African American men behind bars at much faster rate than their counterparts of other races. Quicker convictions and more time. President Obama knew that this was unjust and made a mission to get this handled.

One day as I sat home watching television my phone had rung.

"Hello," I answered.

"Hello, you have a collect call from Steve Collins would you like to except?"

"Yes," I said excited to speak to my brother.

"Hey sis, what's up?". He sounded cheerful. Something was up.

"I'm good just made it in the house from work watching television, how's it going?"

"Good. Listen here, in a few days stay tuned to the news there's some laws that will go retro that President Obama might pass which will lighten my sentence."

"What are you serious Steve? Wait, what does that mean? What's retroactive?" I asked as sat on the edge of the couch.

"Retroactive means, that law will go into effect right away."

"What! Thank you Jesus!," I jumped up and yelled. The biggest smiled came across my face and tears began to fill my eyes.

"Yes, God is good all the time," Steve replied. He sounded hopeful, and that's all I needed. " Listen, just stay on the lookout I'm looking to receive a second chance with a new start. I'm praying sis."

"Steve, I've never stopped praying. God hears our prayers, love you and talk with you in a few days."

I was ecstatic. The news was a blessing, not just for Steve but for many other young men who were serving life-long sentences that were unjustified. It was time the government implemented fair judicial laws, and it would happen sooner than we thought.

On April 22, 2014 I tuned into CNN and it was announce the law was finally passed the mandatory-minimum sentencing for the American prison system. President Obama granted to release about 6,000 inmates. This was great new and I prayed Steve would qualify.

I finally came to terms with how things happened the way they did in our lives. Despite all the trials we endured and the fact that he was in jail, it was a blessing to have my brother alive and well. Unlike so many others who grew up with us, I could still visit him and speak with him whenever he called. We lost so many friends to violence throughout the years, to know that we were not one of them, I felt blessed; I knew God favored us. He had a purpose for us that was not yet fulfilled. I didn't know what it was but I believe one of the biggest reasons was because of our mother. Our mother continuously prayed over our safety. Despite her health condition, and her struggles she always provided us with her love. She was a child of God and for that God kept us. The Spirit was showing me this all these years, but it took until that moment to understand and accept this beautiful truth.

11

PUTTING THINGS BACK TOGETHER

My brother was finally home and back with his family. He was given a second chance at life and provided with the opportunity to move forward and leave what was in the past behind him—something he truly looked forward to doing. My brother stayed with me while he got himself together. The support I was able to assist him with was much needed; there were so many changes in society and technology that Steve had to get accustomed to. Our roles changed and he became my little big brother. Steve was so impressed with the accomplishments I had made and the direction of life I was taking. I was no longer just his little sister, I was an accomplished women.

Life was a blessing and with Steve back home I thought it was only right to celebrate. Steve was big on family and loved to party; knowing this I threw him a barbeque—just like old times. The planning for the party was coming together and I was excited, when it came time to the invite I kept it to a minimum because Steve was still adjusting to society. My brother had always been a people person however reentering society was challenging.

When the day of the barbeque arrived, everything went as planned. It turned out great. I only invited a few of Steve's friends and that was all he needed. It was good to see people we grew up with come by to hang out; yet, seeing them made us realize how many we lost. Steve did eight years out of the twenty-four that he was sentenced; yet, in that eight years a lot changed. He lost several friends to gun violence and his father passed away. One of the biggest changes was how much I changed. His little sister was thinking of a master plan on how to build a legacy for our family. All we ever wanted as kids was to have the best but the best came with a price. Now we were given another chance to start all over—together.

Holidays were always our favorite time of the year for my family and since we were all back together it was only right to spend Christmas at my house. I had bought the biggest Christmas tree and the kids decorated it and hung trinkets throughout the house. This holiday was very special and we wanted it be remembered. Steve being back home brought my mother's livelihood back. She was finally able to come to grips with dealing with her mental health. With the support of both of her children it made a huge difference for the good. Not only were we all back together, we were able to transition from the life we once lived and overcome obstacles that were set before us.

In addition to all of this, I reconnected my father. We spoke more frequently which was a big change for the both of us. Not having my father around was my biggest battle growing up. I needed a father to help lead and guide me especially when it came to men. My relationships were abusive, both mentally and physically—many of which sparked because I would provoke my partner and had a lack of respect for myself. Although Steve was always there for me, I needed to have a father and daughter conversation to express to my dad what I had been through in the past years of my life. I was glad we were able to reconnect. I was no longer just his little girl. I was a woman with a purpose.

12

BUILDING

As the years went by, more opportunities began to present themselves. Before I knew it I was planning events. I partnered with an old friend of mine, Claude. We hosted a few local events together in the city. Our events ranged from comedy, poetry and other forms of entertainment . Our city was small which meant not a lot going on. Because of this we would have hundreds come out to support causing us to gain extreme amounts of exposure throughout the city. As successful as we were, it took some getting used to. I was always well known because of my brother and the guys I dated but I never was the one who wanted to be in front of the camera. I was living a life of sin so I was okay playing the back. Yet, the bigger we became the more I became comfortable with the idea . This business became a lifechanging experience for me. It was a positive movement that attracted a different group of people that I needed to connect with for positive support.

Thanksgiving was right around the corner and Claude and I had an opportunity to host a Comedy Jam. Comedian, Joe Torry, was the headliner. He had starred in some of the greatest movies of all time such as *Poetic Justice* and did skits on *Def comedy Jam*. With an opportunity like this it would be the beginning of our entertainment business. I spent months promoting and selling tickets putting my all in making sure this was a successful event. One thing that never changed about me, I was always ready to make money. When The day of the show arrived, I sold over $18,000 in tickets. The show was well put together and turned out great. This was the beginning to the greatness ahead.

After the show, an organization reached out to me. They invited me to come speak with woman going through rehabilitation. I was confused on where the invitation had come from but it wasn't a surprise since my name had surfaced around the city for my position within the community. The coordinator with this program wanted me to speak on leadership. I had no clue what I would say; I honestly didn't think I was a leader or even knew how to become one. I went on to accept the invite. At that moment, I knew God had intervened in my life. I called my dad to make plans to visit him. It was time for us to see each other face to face so I could fully move on and help others. It had been eighteen long years since we last seen each other in person. but I was ready.

Heading out to California I had so many thoughts going through my head how would he look or say when we come face to face. No matter what, I knew there would be closure. On my way to meet my father, Steve called me wishing me good luck. He reminded me everything in life happens for a reason. No matter what I once felt about my father, some situations are just out of our control. I had to live with the here and now. We talked some more and I thanked him for his words of wisdom.

When I arrived I was nervous as hell but ready. I knew with everything that had happened in my life had a reason for me to be where I was at in that moment. There was no time for pointing fingers to blame and there was no way to replace lost time. The only room left was to move forward and that's exactly what my father and I did.

***

I made it back to Peoria from enjoying my trip with my dad. It was now time to be the guest speaker at the event I was invited to. The moment I walked into the building I still hadn't grasp what I would speak about but I knew it would come to me. As I walked towards the front of the room with about ten women looking directly at me, the spirit shielded me and I heard a voice whisper, *"Empower these women with hope."* I was at a lost but it stuck in my head, *'empower those women with hope.'* I took a deep breath and decided to do just that.

"Hello everyone, and thank you for having me. My name is Alecia Collins and I would like to share with you all today why it's so important to stay encouraged and never give up on self..."

13
EMPOWER OTHERS

2017 was here and it had a whole new meaning to me. I was determined to walk into the new year full with ideas and visions. There was something that picked at me while working and brainstorming with Claude until I could no longer ignore it. I was going to host a Women's Empowerment Seminar. Speaking with that group of women showed me that there was a need in my community. Peoria was listed as one of the worst cities for African Americans to live it. Having this Seminar would change that conversation and be the first of its kind.

With everything I had going on including with running my own business and managing my rental property, I knew this event would consume a lot of my time. When I mentioned it to Claude he wasn't so big on the idea nor thought people would even show up since it was gravitating towards change rather entertainment. However; that didn't faze me. That was my goal—to change up the norm from what people knew of us. I wanted to connect with people on another level and get them involved in their community. Peoria faced many challenges and employment was one of them. I wanted them care more about their health and find financial stability then about the next party.

This seminar would help so many women of all walks of life and my goal was to direct them to services that are available right here in the city. As I connected with different companies while advertising my cleaning service, I was able to meet great women along the way who inspired me to continue to work hard. The idea of having this event wouldn't leave my mind, so instead of waiting for approval I began to make preparation to put it together. I didn't know what direction it would go I just knew I had to put it together and follow through.

I connected with a friend of mine who was also in the entertainment business. She invited me to have dinner with her near Chicago because she wanted to introduce me to a few individuals.. This was an opportunity for me to really get involved and make my vision come to life. When our meeting date arrived, I was ready with pen and paper and a brain full of questions. As I walked into the restaurant and asked for my party the hostess walked me over to our table. When I saw who was sitting there I stopped in my tracks.

"Hello, how are you sweetheart" she said and smiled. It was none other than the talented and beautiful Vivica A. Fox. I was at an awe.

"Great," I nervously responded. "How are you?"

I sat down and I couldn't believe who I was actually having dinner with. I didn't want to waste time so I got right to the point. . Vivica was extremely genuine and laid back, she made me feel very comfortable.

"What's your concept on women empowering women?" I asked.

"We have to uplift and inspire our young women," she

said gracefully. It was simple yet powerful. It was everything I vision about the Women's Seminar. Right then I knew with her attitude she would make a great speaker for the event and as we conversed with one another it was only due time that we would empower women together.

It was very important to keep my meeting with Vivica to myself. While my mind was thinking, my spirit would direct me to those who would be a part of this platform. I would take my life experiences that I had overcome, as topics for each speaker to touch base on. I had lived through so many things that made me stronger. Women today are powerful. We carry the weight of the households and raise our children to the best of our abilities, even at our weakest. This seminar would help women from all walks of life and empower them, encouraging them not to give up.

After months of planning, the moment had come; Claude and I were ready to give the town a different look on life. On July 22, 2017 in Peoria, Illinois the Women Empowering Women Luncheon would take place with Keynote Speaker, Vivica A. Fox, as well as a Host of Influential Speakers. It would be an event to uplift and empower individuals, professionally, financially and spiritually.

The city was excited to know this would happen. Having an A-List celebrity involved gave even more reason for the community to look forward to it. God had placed this vision upon me and my faith to carry through made it happen. I didn't know how much work would be involved and the depths I would go but He prepared me. I set out to make those connections with individuals throughout the state and I was ready.

The day had come and was I ready. My support team

was just as excited as I was; we prepared for the day of the event two nights in advance to make sure everything ran smoothly. It was time to open the doors to share the knowledge of what each influential speaker had to share with each guest. The love in the room flowed from one person to another. The room was anointed with God's grace and mercy. There were over 700 women who came together. The power in the room as we all stood and Welcomed Vivica A. Fox to the city with a round of applause was unmatchable. It all finally came together. And at that moment, I realized this was my purpose.

That day I came to understand why my life was a battle. I had been at war with the enemy that bounded me. It took some time but I was finally set free. And it happened because I held on to faith. My vision came to life and it was because I worked hard and prayed harder. Giving up was never an option.

Claude and I had many ideas of our own and with that we decided to go our separate ways. We had built something in the city of Peoria that would grow and be remembered for years to come. My vision was to move forward and I wanted to become more diverse. What would soon come was my own brand; one which personified my ambition and drive.

Lady A. Entertainment.

14
LADY A. ENTERTAINMENT

Lady A. Entertainment was born and I was excited to bring my ideas to life. I knew that this level of planning would require me to do one event at a time. I wanted my connections to be meaningful—more than just for the sake of entertainment. My next event was, The Beauty Brunch Expo which touched base on the beauty from within as well as provide opportunities for vendors to showcase their items. The guest speakers were women who were well educated and able to connect attendees with resources and help detect the root of their issues. This is so important due to the fact women keep a lot of their problems hidden. This event would give women the opportunity to step out there comfort zone and ask questions to help their situation. The message was simple "Love yourself enough to care how you feel on the inside and the outside will continually shine." Women enjoyed with the delivery of each message the speakers delivered and the one on one connection after the event. The feedback was amazing.

The momentum in the city was at a high it was important for me to gravitate to each class of individuals throughout the city to learn more about my community and study what interested them. My brand would open opportunities for all with creativity and purpose. That was my mission and it still is.

Lady A Entertainment embodied my life mission to help others. I wanted to share my story with my hometown, but also with other who have had similar experiences. It is time to make connections and open doors. That is how we build community. Having the Women Empowerment Seminar was just the beginning. Over time organizations throughout the state of Illinois and other event coordinators reached out, asking for help with bringing their vision to life. Before I knew it, I became an Event Coordinator Consultant.

I continued to throw more events surrounding community and entertainment. One of my other very successful events was my Thanksgiving Comedy Jam. I was honored to connect with a well=known Comedian/Actor Reginald Ballard, better known as "Bruh' Man" from the Fifth floor on the hit sitcom *Martin*. The show turned out great and was very successful. I wanted to show my supporters that Lady A. was versatile. We supported community and made sure you would have a good time. I was finally living out my purpose, and it was all thanks to the Most High.

I had faith and stepped outside the box, doing exactly what the Spirit called me to do. I had to go farther than my belief, and with faith in God I was able to do exceedingly and abundantly well.

In winter 2017, I was contacted by Peoria Magazines inquiring about an interview for their December Subscription. They followed my journey and I was chosen as an Influential Woman in the community. They asked many questions and I always made sure to give my truth. Yes, I am successful but it is important for me to share how I became the humble woman that stands today. To do so, I have to go back to the summer of 1990, in the Northside Peoria where it all began.

I was a small girl with big dreams and little hope. A young girl with a mother who battled schizophrenia; yet, who loved her two children dearly and did the best she could. I had a brother who would play the man of the house and fend for his family by any means necessary. My story is likely like a lot of others but my truth is this: No matter how much you have or how little, always love yourself for who you are.